Lucinda Lambton

VICTORIANA

with a foreword by Sir John Betjeman

ELSEVIER·PHAIDON

To Barnaby and Huckleberry

Acknowledgements

First and foremost, the author would like to thank Sir John Betjeman for his kind words in the Foreword. She is also most grateful to the following people who have given so much of their time, knowledge and advice: Michael Allen, for keeping the cameras in perfect order; Colin Amery for his help; Frank Atkinson for his advice; Julian Barnard for months of research and help; Jacqui Bolton who, by helping so kindly with my children, gave me the freedom needed to work on the book; Carrie Carr, for the unstinted devotion and help given to its writing and typing; John Chessyre, for his kindness and tolerance in the wake of constant questioning; Nicholas Cooper, who at a moment's notice went over the whole manuscript with a fine toothcomb; Dan Cruickshank, who devoted hours of his time to advise and help with the book through its final stages; Jill Downing, who many times took over the running of my household for days on end; Mark Girouard, for parting with his original research without a murmur; Tom Greaves for his valuable advice; Robin Haddow for all his help; Dick Hall, who by initially commissioning articles for *The Observer* started the book on its way; Henry, Barnaby and Huckleberry Harrod, my husband and children, who must have suffered a great deal at the expense of this book but who have never complained; David Mclaughlin and David Rhodes, who showed me the glories of Manchester and gave me hours of their valuable time; the late Jo Riddell and his wife Joan, for ensuring that every photograph was perfect; Sarah Spicer for months of valuable research and who, with her husband Julian, gave excellent advice; Michael Wallis, who has helped so much with the photography; and my father.

Elsevier · Phaidon
an imprint of Phaidon Press Ltd.
Littlegate House,
St. Ebbe's Street, Oxford

First published 1976
© 1976 by Elsevier · Phaidon, Lausanne

ISBN 0 7290 0006 0

Filmset in Great Britain by Jolly & Barber Ltd., Rugby

Printed in Spain by Heraclio Fournier, S.A.

Contents

Foreword

Lucy Lambton has a glorious and exciting eye for architecture. She can pick out the significant detail which conveys the impression of the whole building to which it belongs. She likes the extraordinary. Her photographs are works of art and deserve wide circulation, for they increase our awareness of despised and ignored things around us. Her text is informed and enthusiastic. Her way of looking at things is a way we can all look at them, inspired by her vision. Lucy Lambton leads the way. No town High Street, no suburban high road, no shop, station or public house is dull to an eye like Lucy Lambton's. She brings to an old subject the fresh outlook of youth.

John Betjeman

Introduction

There was a church built to look like a steam engine, with the tower a great funnel; a tomb built as a tent; a carpet factory in Glasgow a glittering Venetian palace; and a tunnel-keeper's house in Sussex was built as a castle around the tunnel entrance. In Sway in Hampshire, Gothic pigsties were built in concrete; in Yorkshire, railway tunnel ventilating shafts present themselves above ground as miniature castellated turrets; there were ornamental dog kennels and henhouses, lamp-posts and letterboxes, pumping stations disguised as fortified medieval manor houses and hospitals built in the style of French Renaissance palaces.

It is this curious side of Victorian architecture that this book aims to reveal: what today seems to us so unexpected, either for its eccentricity alone or for the meticulous care that was taken with every detail.

Elaborate street furnitures, blending into the equally elaborate streetscapes, were so fine that they often became monuments of interest in their own right. Outside St. George's Hall in Liverpool there are fifty-eight dolphin-entwined cast-iron lamp-posts standing elegantly about the stately open piazza, and they themselves produce a visual triumph quite separate from the great Classical pile that they are simply meant to enhance. Public lavatories, too, and milestones, street signs and signposts, all had to a greater or lesser degree the decoration thought to be ideally suitable for their purpose—and also, which is still so important, ideally suitable for their surroundings. A tweed mill in Chipping Norton, Oxfordshire, sits elegantly in a valley, enhancing the landscape with its stone dome and tall chimney wherever it comes into view. In Manchester, block after block of Victorian piles magnificently complement each other. It is the same in Glasgow; there never seems to have been a jarring note in either landscape or townscape.

So it seems to us, that is. In the nineteenth century, industrialization on such a massive scale must have jarred a great deal on many, however finely disguised were its manifestations. John Ruskin was horrified; he declared that iron would cause a 'departure from the first principles of art . . . the tendency of all present sympathy and association is to limit the idea of architecture to non-metallic work.' 'The definition of iron', he said, 'by the

Delphic oracle, calamity upon calamity (meaning iron upon the anvil) has only been in these last days entirely interpreted.'

Expansion on the level that England was now experiencing was making life ever more disagreeable for Ruskin and his contemporaries. 'Arts and Industry', said Walter Crane, 'remain an ill-assorted couple and furnish an additional modern instance to those who rudely ask "is marriage a failure?"' To them it was an appalling failure, producing an ever more commercial existence. 'Commerce, like the old woman in the nursery tale, stands at the sty (of an overstocked market), with the obdurate pig (over-production) that refuses to leave until the stick (of new demand) has been persuaded to bring its influence to bear, and one by one all the characters of the commercial drama act and react upon each other by the very necessities of their existence, so the whole wheel of industrial production is fed and set in motion and grinds on year after year.' To these noble minds, it seemed that the arts were sinking. Ruskin pleaded for architecture to be taught in our schools from Cornwall to Northumberland, as one would teach English spelling and grammar.

Ironically, even those who were in sympathy with the new methods still looked to nature for inspiration. It was a matter that was taken very seriously; Owen Jones, in *The Grammar of*

1. *Above:* life-size stone tent erected in a churchyard at Mortlake, Richmond, Surrey, in memory of Sir Richard Burton, the explorer, by his wife, Isabel, after an elaborate Catholic funeral. Bells originally rang from the inside when they were caught by the breezes. Vandalism has caused it to be bricked up, but it will shortly be restored. The Department of the Environment has allocated £650 to open it up and make the necessary repairs.

2. *Opposite, top:* twisted Jacobean-style chimney of one of the highly decorated cottages of the estate village of Old Warden Park, Bedfordshire. This was built for Lord Ongley in the 1840s, and is thought to have been designed by P. F. Robinson, as he published pattern books in the 1820s showing the same picturesque designs.

3. *Opposite, bottom:* detail of Templeton's carpet factory, Glasgow Green, Glasgow, designed in 1889 by William Leiper (see also Pls. 4 and I).

Ornament, written in 1856, declared: 'There has been a universal cry "Go back to nature as the ancients did" . . . Nature is said to abhor a vacuum . . . It may equally be said that she abhors an angle. In the whole range of her vegetable products it will be impossible to find a line butting on another line; every branch of a tree, every stem upon the leaf is always softened at the point of junction with another by a re-entering curve.' Here he is going beyond the realms of pure decorative detail, as he does regularly in this great tome. When describing a chestnut leaf, he eulogizes again: 'The single example of a chestnut leaf . . . contains the whole of the laws which are to be found in nature. No art can rival the perfect grace of its form, the perfect proportional distribution of the areas, the radiation from the parent stem, the tangential curvatures of the lines, or the even distribution of the surface decoration. We may gather all this from a single leaf.'

In addition to naturalistic decoration, the present book shows many other aspects of Victorian architecture. It deals with industrial buildings, municipal buildings, great houses, villas and terraces, each as elaborate as the next; with railway stations, whose architects explored every imaginable style; with street furniture, which played such an integral part in the townscape; with gravestones, whose emotional associations led to boundless flights of fancy; with public houses, restaurants and hotels, whose success depended on their extravagant decoration; and lastly with shops, whose charm and originality are now disappearing before our very eyes.

Often not of superlative architectural quality, but nearly always of superlative architectural charm, it was the bits and pieces, great and small, that made the visual quality of Victorian life so high. The attitude that every building, whatever it was, merited the greatest care and attention is epitomized by John Claudius Loudon in his massive tome, *The Encyclopedia of Cottage, Farm and Villa Architecture and Furniture,* written in 1833. It gives a mass of advice on detail: 'Chimney tops are features of considerable importance', begins one chapter—a school of thought for which we can be grateful today, when we find some twisted barley-sugar-stick chimney pot, complete with its castellated top, still unchanged. Six pots were illustrated in the *Encyclopedia*, all elaborate examples of the 'Italian' style, and one with an angel puffing smoke from its mouth. 'Window dressings are fine sources of character', said Loudon, and 'may be ornamented in a great variety of ways.' Barge-boarding, verandas, terrace parapets, balconies, porches and doorways, all are discussed and exquisitely illustrated. For a Gothic dairy it is suggested that: 'In the centre of the angles formed by the arches supporting the slate shelves are fastened small rams' heads. These internal decorations give . . . an air of finish and taste.'

4. *Opposite:* detail of Templeton's carpet factory, Glasgow Green, Glasgow (see also Pls. 3 and I). 'Nothing finer is to be found outside of Italy', said the designer's junior partner, W. H. McNab. The future of this magnificent building is now uncertain, as the business has expanded to two new premises on the south side of the city and it has not yet been decided whether or not to keep the factory at Glasgow Green.

Great circular stables are illustrated, to be built in either the 'Tudor Gothic' or the 'Italian' style, both with central bell towers. A vast gateway is also proposed, some 40 feet high, adorned with twelve life-size (if not larger than life-size) animals: two stags, two does, a wolf, a leopard, a lion, a fox, a monkey, a goat, a bear and a wild boar. This was thought to be suitable for 'a garden containing a zoological collection'! Designs for 'the requisite accommodations for kennels for sporting dogs' were considered to be ideal, again, in either the 'Tudor Gothic' or the 'Italian' style. Both had semi-circular entrance porches, the first with an ornate series of arches, the second with a grand pillared arcade. For farm buildings, the Gothic style is suggested, with buttresses and parapets, 'and a moderately high roof'.

The money was there for all these extravagances, and there were spirited imaginations to utilize it. The carpet factory in Glasgow, built as a dazzling Venetian Gothic palace and mentioned earlier, has twisted ceramic pillars, patterned yellow and red brickwork, brick carvings, and blue, turquoise and gold mosaics. It still stands on Glasgow Green, hard to believe in, but quite extraordinarily beautiful.

The gentlemen's lavatory in the glittering Philharmonic public house in Liverpool has marble urinal stalls and a marble cistern, decorated tiled walls and brass taps on the two marble washbasins, which are supported by cast-iron angels. At Eastcheap in London, on the corner of Philpot Lane, there is, unexpectedly jutting out all around the parapet of a not particularly distinguished building, an elaborate frieze, consisting of over forty stone heads of hunting dogs and wild boars.

In Leeds there are two factories which stand within a few streets of each other; one, enormous and black, is an Egyptian palace, on the roof of which whole flocks of sheep were put out on cultivated pastures to provide the company with wool. From the other rise two chimneys, each a perfect replica of a sixteenth-century Italian campanile, complete with perfectly proportioned windows. Standing there, one thinks for all the world that one is in Italy, but then they are strangely dark and dirty, covered with thick layers of grime.

If you search, such delights can still be found all over Britain. In London, go to Kensal Rise Cemetery to see the enchanting variety of tombs, sculptured stone ponies, babies, soldiers, anchors and armchairs, women and children. Go to Ipswich in Suffolk for a splendidly ornate fish shop, decorated throughout with tiles, individually designed for its owner; to Gosport in Hampshire for one of the most beautiful and stately of British railway stations, now in a sad state of decay; to Liverpool for spectacular great public houses, the best in England. Look at the elaborate drainpipe brackets on York Station Hotel; a mile or two away at Great

5. *Opposite:* Italian campanile factory chimneys of the Tower Works, Globe Road, Leeds. The one on the left was modelled, by Thomas Shaw in 1864, on the Lamberti tower in Verona. The other, a chimney for the brickworks' dust extractor plant, with gilded tiled panels inset into the windows, was based on Giotto's tower in Florence by William Bakewell in 1899.

Ayton, a cast-iron urinal still stands, with a charming little head on the gutter spouting water from its mouth. Go to Papplewick in Nottingham for a gleaming palace of a pumping station; to Rendcomb in Gloucestershire for horses' heads carved above the stable yard, entwined with stone ribbons, roses, corn, tulips, peas, convolvulus and daisies.

Such pleasures can still be enjoyed, but many may well not be with us for much longer.

6. Horse's head carved over the archway into the stableyard of Rendcomb, Gloucestershire. Both the stables, including the enormous clock tower over this arch, and the house to which they belong were designed in 1865 by P. C. Hardwick.

Decorative Detail

At Morwenstow in Cornwall in 1860, the poet Robert Stephen Hawker built a vicarage for himself with five out of its six chimneys made as replicas of his favourite church towers. 'The sixth perplexed me very much', said Hawker, 'till I bethought me of my mother's tomb; and there it is in its exact shape and dimensions' (Barbara Jones, *Follies and Grottoes*, 1953). This delightful example illustrates perfectly the curious charm of so much of nineteenth-century architecture and the Victorians' extravagant passion for detail. They felt that the purpose of building was to please the eye and to stimulate the senses: 'Architecture proposes an effect on the human mind, not merely a service to the human frame', wrote Ruskin. Decoration was seen as an ideal course to follow: 'Architecture is the art which so disposes and adorns the edifices raised by man for whatsoever uses, that the sight of them may contribute to his mental health, power and pleasure' (Ruskin again). Adornment, therefore, was part of architecture and the greater the building the greater the adornment. But as social aspirations wound their way through the whole of British society, the visible parts of every structure flourished, so that the grandest town hall was emulated by the humblest terrace house. The Victorians proclaimed through their buildings the solidarity of their new-found wealth, their technical prowess, their new materials, and above all their high ideals. And hospitals, libraries, arcades, public houses, swimming pools, fire stations, factories, hotels and public lavatories were all given the same intense care and consideration.

Splendid new machine-made embellishments had allowed these ideals to become an economic reality, and even the most modest homes had a rich variety of enchanting porches, stained-glass windows, ornamental chimneys, gargoyles or pinnacled roofs, brick-patterned walls and pillared doors. In the district of Fulham, London, some 2000 lions sit proudly on the gables of houses in endless rows, 3 or 4 to each roof, and many more sit below on elaborately carved balconies. This same development starts up again two miles away in Barnes. In another everyday street in Hammersmith, rows of stone pillars with elaborately carved capitals hold up the porches or decorate the bay windows, and each

8. *Above:* detail of the decorative tiling in the Shanghai ward of the old Charing Cross Hospital, London, S.W.1., which is no longer in use. Part of the 1881 extension to the original 1831 Decimus Burton buildings, this ward has a series of tiled tableaux of farmyard scenes, which were hand painted, mostly in different shades of brown, white and cream, by Mr. Simpson of St. Martin's Lane.

9. *Right:* nineteenth-century wooden porch of a small village house in Nettlecomb, Somerset.

7. *Opposite:* Thorntons Arcade, Briggate, Leeds. There is a clock at one end, manned by four life-size mechanical men, and a decorative plaque of a lady in a feathered hat at the other.

one is totally different: arum lilies, domestic and wild strawberries, figs, ferns and chestnut leaves with conkers, ivy and holly; and in the middle of some doorways curious heads appear: a turbaned Indian, a king, a baby, an ear-ringed Negro. This degree of decoration was everyday practice, machine-made perhaps, but at least the trouble was taken to vary the designs, thereby creating an individual building with every home.

The feeling for such naturalistic forms was a dominant force in these high-minded Victorian ideals. Whether because their new-found city lives compared ill with their old rural existence, or perhaps just because of the very perfection that nature does indeed possess, its forms, in one way or another, were far more widely used in decoration than anything else.

'Nature, . . . held up as a beacon light, has flashed conviction and astonishment to many of his votaries, who before trusted to the glimmering rays reflected from a past inspiration', wrote John Pollard Seddon, an architect, in 1852. His book, *Progress in Art and Architecture with Precedents for Ornament*, like that of Owen Jones quoted above, advocated, in the most richly sentimental terms, that nature was the finest source from which to draw for architectural inspiration. The architect, 'in striving to embody some thoughts gathered from the storehouse of Nature, for the

10. *Above:* the window of a one-time lodge of Ettington Park, near Newbold-on-Stour, Gloucestershire, showing the 'ribboning' effect in lead and glass. Dating from 1869, the 'ribbons' are of green coloured glass, while the rest of the panes are plain.

11. *Opposite:* nineteenth-century castellated chimneys, designed by the Rev. Dr. W. K. W. Chafy, of Rous Lench Court, Rous Lench, Worcestershire, which dates from the sixteenth century. It was bought in 1876 by Dr. Chafy, who greatly restored the house and everything else on the estate (see also Pl. X).

instruction and pleasure of generations to come', should 'lay to heart . . . yea, broider it on his very garment' that the unity of nature with architecture 'is the strength'. It was Seddon who designed a massive Gothic tower, twice the height of Big Ben and at least four times the ground area, to stand near Westminster Abbey as part of a scheme to house its overflowing monuments; the project was abandoned only because of its exorbitantly high cost. Richly pinnacled, with open vaulting against the sky ('Gothic is more elaborate the nearer it reaches heaven', according to Sir John Betjeman), it would have rivalled the most skyscraping of skyscrapers today.

During the second half of the nineteenth century such immense projects were constantly translated into grandiose realities, symbols of the great prosperity brought about by the Industrial Revolution. Town halls, museums, libraries, hospitals and banks all had to be built to meet the clamouring need of the newly discriminating public. Social progress was often measured in terms of such schemes, creating in many cases completely new types of buildings. The scale and variety of architecture involved was without precedent and many great men emerged to design and create these new emblems of power. Sir Joseph Bazalgette, for instance, designed the whole sewage disposal system of London,

13. *Opposite:* Foster's Almshouses Colston Street, Bristol, designed in 1861 by architects Foster and Wood. The decoration is highly elaborate, with diaper-patterned brickwork, statues in niches, 'candle snuffer' roofs, ornamental turrets, projecting corner oriels and open spiral staircases.

12. *Below:* detail of the Camelia House, Nettlecomb, Somerset. This was a mass-produced package conservatory, made of timber and glass with ornamental wooden ventilating strips. It was reputedly built in the 1880s as part of the pleasure gardens of Nettlecomb House, which were laid out in 1875. Since the photograph was taken this huge decaying structure has collapsed. According to an eye witness, in the middle of a violent storm it 'rose from the ground, filled with air like a crinoline, and fell, smashing into a thousand pieces'.

which was completed by 1866, the superb Abbey Mills pumping station, in 1865–8, and, between 1864 and 1870, the Victoria Embankment. Another, John Claudius Loudon, whose work was mentioned earlier, was an architect of note, as well as a landscape gardener, a pioneer of agricultural education and the compiler of a complete reference book on domestic architecture (see p. 12). In this book (*The Encyclopaedia of Cottage, Farm and Villa Architecture and Furniture*) there were no fewer then 2342 suggested designs, the introduction of which was intended to 'improve the dwellings of the great mass of society, in the temperate regions of both hemispheres: a secondary object is to create and diffuse among mankind, generally, a taste for architectural comforts and beauties', since architecture 'is the only fine art open to the inspection of all and interesting to all; and could we only succeed in raising the taste of the mass of society in this art, we should not only affect a universal improvement in Architecture, but materially contribute towards the universal adoption of correct and elegant habits of thinking and acting generally.'

Sir Horace Jones (1819–87) was another important figure. He built the superbly solid yet delicately designed Tower Bridge, as well as Smithfield Market, the Guildhall Library, Billingsgate Market, the Guildhall School of Music, and the very beautiful

14. *On previous opening:* Leadenhall Market, Gracechurch Street, London E.C.3., built between 1879 and 1881 by Sir Horace Jones, architect to the City of London. It forms a cross of highly decorated glass-roofed arcades with a great dome in the centre. The construction of the arcades cost some £98,000, and a further £148,000 was spent on making suitable approach roads.

16. *Above:* William Bliss and Son tweed mills, Chipping Norton, Oxfordshire. This was rebuilt in 1872 when the original mill was burnt down. The architect was George Woodhouse of Bolton, Lancashire.

15. *Opposite:* Witley Court, Great Witley, Worcestershire. Originally built in the early eighteenth century for Lord Foley, it was drastically altered in 1838 when the first Earl of Dudley turned it into a palace for entertaining Queen Adelaide. In 1860 it was remodelled by Samuel Dawkes and the gardens, with the great Perseus fountain by J. Forsyth, were laid out by the William Nesfields, father and son (see also Pl. IX). The house was gutted by fire in 1937 and everything is now in ruins.

Leadenhall Market, all in London. The list could be endlessly extended. James Bunstone Bunning (1802–63) rose high above many with the design of the astonishingly beautiful Coal Exchange (so viciously and unnecessarily demolished in 1962). Sixty feet in diameter, a great cast-iron rotunda rose up above three floors of painted galleries. A cable motif was used for the encircling balustrades, and exquisitely painted panels, showing miners with their families, scenes at the pithead and underground, and various leaves and trees fossilized into coal, surrounded by all manner of decorative fantasies, stood regularly spaced round the full height of each gallery. The floor was made up from 4000 pieces of wood of various kinds, representing a mariner's compass with a City of London shield and an anchor in the centre, and the ground-floor walls were decorated in the same way as the galleries.

Bunning also planned Nunhead Cemetery in South London, built several London streets, as well as Holloway prison and the Caledonian Market, and he was often called upon to decorate the capital on special and state occasions. His end was a sad one, on just such a commission. Worn out and over-excited after working for days and nights on decorations to mark the future Princess of Wales' entrance into the City of London in 1862, he was struck down with gastric fever on the very day that the Princess passed under his triumphal arches, and died some months later.

Alfred Waterhouse with his palace of Manchester Town Hall; Gilbert Scott with the stately St. Pancras Hotel in London; Burges with the glorious fantasies of Cardiff Castle and the Tower House, Melbury Road, London; George Edmund Street with the sombre London Law Courts he never lived to see finished: these men were just a few of the great figures that led the way, and many lesser architects followed their example.

Even farm buildings received their share of attention, though an issue of *The Building News* in 1863 contains a report about an ill that we know only too well today. Under the heading 'A Cheap Material For Farm Buildings' one finds, 'A farm has recently been erected at Abbott's Roding, . . . the plan includes the usual buildings . . . barn, stables, cart lodge, granary, cow-house, sheds, piggeries, etc.; and its only peculiarity is that the walls are all formed of concrete blocks.' A 'convenient housestead of a very durable character' had been built, at a saving of over £200; thus 'the substitution of concrete blocks for brickwork may be of service'. However, the Victorians' feeling and spirit for design could even be wrought into concrete. A certain A. T. T. Peterson, who was once a High Court judge in Calcutta, built a slender Indian Gothic tower in pre-cast blocks, some 218 feet high, at Sway in Hampshire. It still stands there today, and very peculiar it is, too, in that

17. *Above:* Smithfield Market, in the City of London. This was built in 1866–7 by Sir Horace Jones, who also designed Leadenhall and Billingsgate Markets. The site of Smithfield was originally open public ground on the borders of the City, where fairs, markets, executions and other public events took place. The cattle market was transferred to the Caledonian Market in 1852.

18. *Opposite:* one of six carved female heads in roundels on the walls of Massey Chambers, 6 Booth Street, Manchester. This building was designed by Edward Solomons in 1872.

although in an Eastern and delicate style, it is constructed in heavy concrete.

The great pile of Waddesdon Manor in Buckinghamshire—a re-creation of a French château—thought by a contemporary to be 'out of harmony with its rural surroundings . . . too new and too grand, it asserts itself overmuch' (James John Hissey, *Across England in a Dog Cart*, 1891), has some exquisitely carved brick on its farmyard buildings. Above an archway a great bull stands with a cow and calf, a farmworker and two sheep. Beyond, fields roll off to a distant church and village. On the walls of one of the farm cottages processions of haycarts are carved in panels. A cowshed at Welbeck in Nottinghamshire has been given grandiose classic elegance, with enormous pierced stone balls decorating its roof. The same estate's poultry run is flanked by huge stone birds on pillars. A timbered estate village, Walsham-le-Willows in Suffolk, has pious sayings carved into its beams—'As man lives, so he shall die'.

John Claudius Loudon had high hopes for 'farmery' architecture. His dream that the farm building, even when on a larger, more industrial scale, could still beautify the land is stirringly defined in his *Encyclopaedia*—and one could as well apply his words to factories and mills. After announcing that 'nothing disfigures the country more than red-brick chimney shafts', Loudon goes on to speak of superior examples that did exist. One in Birmingham was thought to be ideal, and another in Glasgow 'a good example . . . both for the remarkable elegance of the shafts, or obelisks, and the happy termination by which ornament is given'. He goes on:

> Could a few such shafts as those be introduced . . . the effect in the landscape would be excellent. It is only necessary to imagine them, as the traveller moves along the public road, rising into view one after another, on the prominencies of the plains, and on the cultivated sides of the hills . . . Perhaps the time may come, when, from almost every large farmer being the proprietor of the land he occupies, there will be a competition among them as to who shall erect the handsomest shafts, similar to what there was in former ages among the Catholic clergy as to the building of spires to their churches and monasteries. Like the spires and towers of churches, the column and the obelisk are forms that, though without variety in themselves, yet, when high, and elegantly proportioned, never tire in the general view, however often they may be repeated. We strongly recommend the subject to the attention of Architects. The public have surely a right to expect that such conspicuous objects as engine chimney-shafts are, in the country should be built in what is considered good taste, no less than the spires of churches.

19. *Opposite:* Watts Warehouse, 35–47 Portland Street, Manchester. Now known as Britannia House, this was designed in 1851 by Travis and Mangnall and has an elaborately balustraded central stair-well which extends to the full height of the building (see also Pl. VIII). For many years it was threatened with demolition, but it is now safe and renovation, which promises to be very successful, is being carried out.

Noble words, and words that were so much part of the atmosphere that surrounded the Victorians and their architecture. Such spires and towers were actually built; the stately beauty of the tweed mills at Chipping Norton bears witness to the dream of Loudon and others becoming a reality, as does the four-towered keep of Stoke Newington pumping station, the water tower at Grimsby, the turreted warehouse of Newcastle Breweries, the hexagonal and castellated Victoria Tower at the entrance to Salisbury Dock in Liverpool, and many other such monuments to industry and taste. Every detail, however unimportant it may seem to us, was carefully considered, and the workmanship was always superb; for instance, bronze cranes swathe the capitals of the pillars supporting the engine-room at Papplewick pumping station in Nottinghamshire and little iron fish swim up the columns through iron water irises. The brass handle and keyhole covers inside and out are details of perfection. Great iron hinges decorate the front door, and a little staircase inside, made up of section upon section of iron cast as giant petals, climbs up on a panelled oak support. Designed by Ogle Tarbotton, and built between 1881 and 1885, the whole is an example of craftsmanship of the highest order.

It has been suggested that the Victorians shied away from functionalism and sought to disguise everything with a rich covering of embellishment. This criticism surely looks at their decoration in the wrong light; the spirit and exuberance with which adornment was executed shows that it was there for its own sake alone, art merging with architecture to emphasize their all-important original source, nature. 'Architecture alone, sculpture and painting alone, individually, are incapable of the full rendering of the majesty of nature; it is by the union of their several efforts alone that her whole excellence can be declared', wrote John Pollard Seddon. He was voicing the ideals of his age.

I. *Opposite:* detail of Templeton's carpet factory, Glasgow Green, Glasgow, designed in 1889 by William Leiper (see also Pls. 3 and 4). Its vast size, its Venetian Gothic style (complete with Guelfic battlements), and its colours—the terracotta red, the multi-coloured glazed brickwork, the blue mosaic, the gold, green and browns—make it a very curious sight in Glasgow.

II. *Overleaf:* 23–25 Eastcheap (originally Nos. 38–39), London E.C.3., designed as a warehouse for Messrs. Hunt and Crombie and as showrooms for colonial produce by architects John Young & Son of King Street, Cheapside. The frieze of hunting dogs and wild boars was made by architectural sculptors Messrs. Nettle and Sarson of Westminster Road. Down the side of the building, at street level, a small carved mouse can be seen, eating cheese. It was carved by the workmen in honour of a mouse that was always eating their lunch. The whole block will shortly be demolished. It is to be developed by the City of London Real Property Company into offices, shops and a car park.

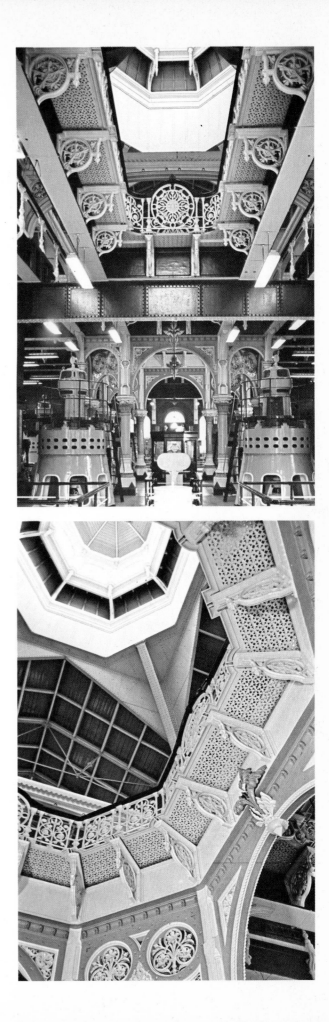

II, IV. *Opposite:* Rylands Library, Deansgate,
Manchester, designed in 1899 by Basil Champneys for
Euriqueta Augustina Rylands as a memorial to her
husband, the great philanthropist John Rylands. The
Gothic ecclesiastical style is presumably due to it
having been originally a theological library. *Above
left:* 60 Pell Road, Reading. Dating from the early 1900s
and built of red brick with deep white-brick dressings
to the windows and quoins, this house is in one street
amongst many in Reading with such elaborately
patterned brickwork.

V, VI. *Above right and right:* Abbey Mills pumping
station, Abbey Lane, Stratford, London E.C.15. This
was built in 1865–8 by Sir Joseph Bazalgette as part of
his scheme for the main drainage of London. Inside
there are two levels of ornate ironwork with pillars,
decorative arches, brackets, overhead balustrades, and
balconies where even the grilles underfoot are cast as
little petalled flowers within circles.

VII, VIII. *Overleaf, left:* Papplewick pumping station,
8 miles north of Nottingham. Built between 1881 and
1885 by Ogle Tarbotton, engineer, the cost of
constructing this splendid building, with its 120-foot-
high tower and ornamental ponds which could hold
1,381,000 gallons of water, was £64,000. *Overleaf, right:*
Watts Warehouse, Manchester, built in 1851 by Travis
and Mangnall (see also Pl. 19).

IX. *On previous opening:* the orangery at Witley Court, Great Witley, Worcestershire. A thirteen-bay, Italianate structure, it was presumably built when the new gardens were laid out in 1860 (see Pl. 15).

XII. *Opposite:* two of the fifty-eight dolphin-entwined lamps of the 1850s on St. George's Plateau in front of St. George's Hall in Liverpool. These were removed in the early 1950s for conversion to electricity, and replaced by the blackened perspex globes there today. On the steps of St. George's Hall in front of the pillared portico, is the statue of the Earl of Beaconsfield, K.G. (1804–81).

X, XI. *Left:* a letterbox at Rous Lench, Worcestershire (1871)—one of the two designs by the Rev. Dr. W. K. W. Chafy (see Pl. 11), the other being broader but of the same Tudor style. *Below:* the 'Liverpool Special', 1863, on the corner of Church Road and Edge Lane, Liverpool. It was designed by Mr. Gay, the district surveyor. This has disappeared since the photograph was taken in 1972.

XIII. *Opposite, top:* Gosport Station, Hampshire, 1841, designed by Sir William Tite. The fourteen-bay Tuscan colonnade, with a square pavilion at the east end, is now decaying and overgrown. The County Architect has estimated that to retain this structure as a ruin would cost £12,000, with an annual upkeep of a further £2,000. The Gosport Borough Council would like to make the site into a formal garden, with the station as a decorative ruin.

XV. *Above left:* the outstanding Ionic-columned classical façade of Newmarket Old Station, Cambridgeshire, 1848. The owners, Finsbury Developments Ltd., have planning permission to build thirty-three houses on the 2·4 acre site, but with the stipulation that the station building must be retained and converted into a public house or some other approved use.

XVI, XVII. *Above right:* Wateringbury Station, Kent, 1844. This was adapted from a house on the line by William Cubitt, engineer to the line (see also Pl. 43). *Below:* detail of the fireplace in the royal waiting-room at Windsor, Eton and Riverside Station, Berkshire. Dating from 1851, this station was designed by Sir William Tite (see also Pls. 39 and 40).

XIV, XVIII. Liverpool Street Station, London. *Opposite, bottom:* view down the central colonnade of this great terminus, designed in 1874–5 by Edward Wilson, an engineer. It was built on a cathedral plan, with isles, chancel and a nave, which is crossed by a transcept. *Overleaf:* the 1894 extension by Edward Wilson's son, John, and W. N. Ashbee.

Street Furniture

Whatever one's taste, one cannot deny to the Victorians the triumph of producing aesthetically integrated streetscapes, which were designed carefully as such, without any of the jarring intrusions that seem to be typical of the street scenes of today.

Lamp-posts, bollards, street signs, milestones, benches, railings—while being given their full due as important visual media in their own right—were designed as an integral part of the streetscape. Despite their diversity, they welded the city together, as it were, producing a complete unit of design.

Even letterboxes managed to appear in twenty different guises. It was Anthony Trollope, curiously, who first introduced them into England. He was then a surveyor's clerk for the Post Office and in charge of improving the postal service in Jersey. In 1851 he suggested trying out a scheme for the posting of letters like that in use in France at the time, '. . . all that is wanted is a safe receptacle for letters . . . Iron posts suited for the purpose may be erected at the corner of streets in such situations as may be desirable.' By 1852 four had been erected in St. Helier. They were immediately successful. Two months later the postmaster of St. Helier wrote: 'The roadside letterboxes . . . work satisfactorily . . . I feel assured that their introduction into England would be followed by most beneficial results . . . but there they must be introduced liberally and energetically, and with fitting modifications as to size, form and make.'

They were indeed introduced liberally and energetically, and with a great many modifications as to size, form and make; there were fluted hexagonal pillars, massive cylindricals and graceful narrow ones, some had six sides, some were highly decorated, others completely plain. The 'Hexagonal Penfold' appeared in 1857, so-called because its designer was a Mr. J. W. Penfold. Six-sided, it was embossed with a royal coat of arms above the aperture, a decorated cornice, cast-iron leaves in relief on its roof and a shapely spike. Quite a few of these still survive—more often than not, though, without their pinnacle.

An amusing mistake was made in 1856 when, due to confusion over the instructions given by the designer, three immensely high

XIX. *Opposite:* cast-iron pillars with naturalistic capitals supporting a platform canopy at Great Malvern Station, Worcestershire, 1859, by E. W. Elmslie (see also Pl. 46). There are fourteen pillars on each of the two platforms; some of the designs of the capitals are repeated three times, others twice. They were repainted in the original strong, clear colours in 1970 by a retired British Rail employee.

49

domed pillar boxes were cast in Birmingham. They were splendid fluted columns with steep domes surmounted by enormous crowns, and stood 8 feet high. So as not to hurt anyone's feelings, one was placed in New Street Station, but it is doubtful whether many people used it as its aperture was 7 feet from the ground. Sadly it is no longer there. In Liverpool a Mr. Gay, the district surveyor, showed great spirit in designing his own box. Huge and round, it too was surmounted by a great ornate crown. It is interesting to note that until 1874 all letterboxes were painted green. The process of re-painting, done only when each box needed it anyway, took ten years.

It was iron, of course, and the increased use of 'cast iron'—which could be melted and cast into a mould—that made the great mass production of street furniture possible. Wrought iron, its predecessor, could be forged, rolled and shaped, but not cast into a mould, and was therefore never produced on such a scale. McFarlane's of Glasgow, in their castings catalogue of 1874, give us an idea of the richness of decoration that could now appear everywhere. The frontispiece illustrates the showroom, a splendid cast-iron pillared gallery with each bracket, capital and column different, displaying a fairyland of interweaving shapes and patterns. There are fountains, railings, bandstands, gates, lamps,

50

drinking troughs, fishscaled glass and iron canopies (one can still be seen at Gosport), floor gratings and arches. The skyline is extraordinary, with domes, crowns, pinnacles, human figures and weathervanes all rising up together. None can be separated yet each one is different.

In this catalogue there are no fewer than 1,425 patterns of ornamental railings, 114 of ornamental drainpipe heads, 475 of ornamental gutters and 773 of terminals for roofs. 'There is, perhaps, no section of our manufactures', said Walter McFarlane & Co., 'that better illustrates the vast improvements we have introduced in ornamental castings than our Terminals, imparting, as they do, refreshing points of interest to the architecture, at a comparatively trifling cost. The wide range of designs in our Terminals, and other Sections, gives facilities for an endless variety of combinations, suited to every taste and requirement.'

In a section entitled 'Panels and Gratings. For Ventilation, light, view, protection, and ornament', 486 patterns of 'rectangular panels' are shown, all unbelievably elaborate, cast into every imaginable pattern that could be thought pleasing to the eye. And this was simply for the decoration of a ventilator opening or of the grating covering some pipe 'where openings for the passage of heat, light and air are desirable, as in partitions, ceilings, fan-

2. Examples of nineteenth-century street signs, which vary in style from town to town: *top left*, Walsall Rd., Walsall, Warwickshire; *top right*, Town Gate, Pudsey, Yorkshire; *centre left*, Hollybush Row, Oxford; *centre right*, Sheep Street, Charlbury, Oxfordshire; *bottom left*, Plough & Harrow Rd., Birmingham; *bottom right*, Palm Grove, Birkenhead.

3-6. Examples of nineteenth-century cast-iron milestones. *Opposite, top:* very large milestone, with three pointing hands, at Kidderminster in Worcestershire. *Opposite, bottom:* detail of a large milestone, which has two pointing hands (only one of which is shown here), between Evesham and Moreton-in-the-Marsh, Gloucestershire. *Above:* milestone in County Durham, unusual in that it is painted white on black rather than the reverse. *Right:* milestone at Thirsk in Yorkshire which was forged in memory of a local drover.

27, 28. *Above:* detail of one of a
number of benches supported by
cast-iron camels along the Victoria
Embankment, London, which was
opened in 1870. It was designed as
a whole by Sir Joseph Bazalgette,
and other benches are supported
by sphinxes. There are also many
dolphin-entwined lamps with
spherical globes. *Left:* cast-iron
railings and a footscraper at 104
Kensington Church Street,
London W.8., *c.* 1855.

lights, doors, closets, gates, shop windows, etc., and where it is also necessary to protect such openings to prevent the entrance of thieves or vermin.' There are 64 circular panels, all for the same use, 36 semi-circular and 2 triangular, 18 air bricks (also all in different patterns), and 77 floor gratings. To give a random example of the varieties: among the 36 semi-circular panels, there is Queen Victoria, a quatrefoil, a fleur-de-lis, and a cart-wheel; among the rectangular panels: fish scales alternately filled with fleurs-de-lis and cherries, honeycombs within each other, heraldic lions flanking roses, shamrocks, and thistles. There were eagles, too, as well as foliage, berries and a variety of portcullises.

Drainpipes had a further set of totally different designs: 'The important position which these occupy, and the enhanced character and style they impart to a building, give considerable scope for variety of design . . . Crests, Monograms, Dates, etc., can be cast to order.' There were winged griffons, busts of Britannia and castellated turrets. Pattern number 19 is in the highest Gothic: a tiny building on top of the drainpipe, with elaborate terminals sticking up at either end of the fishscaled tiled roof, and curious little seals with bird's beaks slithering down its sides. Most of the rest of these drainpipe heads, although each different from the other, appear to be ornate miniature pulpits at which a miniature priest might well appear, having climbed up by way of the ecclesiastical 'pipe connection'. These were like little Gothic church porches in which the pipes connected under the pointed fishscaled tiled roof.

It is intensely pleasurable to study these designs, but also very depressing, highlighting as they do our present-day attitude to the design of such architectural appendages. Whole vistas are now being ruined daily by the indiscriminate and tasteless intrusions of modern street furniture. Nineteenth-century ornamental lamps, which in many cases could be converted from gas, are being wrenched from the ground in favour of streamlined characterless posts, too often fitting ill into their surroundings. In Bedford Park, London, England's first garden suburb (by Norman Shaw, E. Godwyn and E. J. May) that was begun in 1875 and finished in the first decade of the twentieth century, there is a particularly good example of how this can happen. The streetscape is complete, and was designed to be so by the architects. From the wooden fences or brick walls around the front gardens, up to the balconies and on up to the variety of different gables, there is a soothing melody of red brick and white paint. Trees line the pavements, and the vistas change slightly round each bend. Every few yards, though, a hideous scar gashes into the pleasing street scene: great modern lamp-posts in an unpleasant shade of pale green, always dirty, with white conical globes and nasty little golden Japanese hats, march along the pavement, ruining the whole concept of Bedford Park's original design.

Some lighting departments, however, have made valiant efforts. In York, in the 1930s, when the thin copper of the lanterns of the ornate Gothic posts on Skeldergate and Lendal bridges corroded, they were completely remade to their original pattern, and in Liverpool all fifty-eight of the dolphin-entwined lamps on St. George's Plateau were retained when they were converted to electricity in the 1950s. The original glass globes had to go, but they were sensitively replaced by the black perspex ones that we see today.

Another great extravagance of the Victorians in their schemes for street decoration was the abundance of statues and memorials. The death of Prince Albert in 1861 produced many of these—it seemed that every town and every city throughout the country wanted to raise funds for some tribute to the Queen's late Consort. In Manchester, the committee dealing with the problem took nine months, from January to September 1862, to decide what memorial would be most suitable. Throughout the consideration of the suggestions, which included public baths, a museum, a new cathedral tower and an orphanage, one obligation stood out clearly—that a statue be included in whatever design was chosen. Thomas Worthington finally produced the plan that was thought to be the most worthy: a 'medieval shrine' to cover the prince. It was described in *The Builder* to be 'of that period of medieval architecture which

29, 30. *Above left:* letterbox in Bridge Street, Banbury, Oxfordshire, 1856. This design was used for only a year before a modified version with a horizontal aperture was introduced in 1857. Since the photograph was taken, this fluted letterbox has been removed to the Banbury Museum in Marlborough Road. *Above right:* an 'early mainland' letterbox in Double Street, Framlingham, Suffolk, 1856. This and a similar box on Saxtead Road were made by Handyside & Co. of Derby.

31. *Above:* a glass and cast-iron canopy with a semi-circular hood, dating from 1847, which was originally at St. Vincent Barracks, Forton Road, Gosport, Hampshire. The whole of these barracks, with the exception of the entrance arch, has been demolished to make way for a school, but the canopy was saved and has been re-erected outside the wardroom at H.M.S. Collingwood.

prevailed in Florence between the ages of Giotto and Brunelleschi'. It was and still is a splendid structure, whose fate at the time of writing hangs in the balance, and it led the way for Sir Gilbert Scott to produce his 'piece of monumental jewellery', the Albert Memorial in London. Scott always claimed otherwise, saying that his was a totally new concept reached after much 'painfull' effort. But as it was produced a full fifteen months after Worthington's masterpiece, what conclusions can one draw?

Manchester's memorial, now blackened and corroded by soot, was also an elaborate jewel. Figures representing music, chemistry, mechanics, sculpture, literature and many more are carved beneath the statue, and in addition there are medallions of Beethoven, Milton, Inigo Jones, Shakespeare, Sir Christopher Wren and others.

Queen Victoria, too, appears all over the country—old, young, fat, thin, beautiful and ugly. In Ripon, Yorkshire, on the clock tower, she is a grotesque, wizened little creature, whose hideous appearance is not improved by streaks of dripping birds' lime. In contrast, in St. George's Plateau, Liverpool, there is a beautiful equestrian statue of the Queen in riding habit, with an enchanting feathered bowler on her head and a long elegant switch in her hand.

32. *Opposite:* lamp-posts on Skeldergate Bridge, York, 1878–81. This was designed by Thomas Page and modified after his death by his son George. The bridge was reconstructed in 1938–9 and the copper lanterns replaced by exact replicas.

33, 34. *Overleaf, left:* detail of the clock tower in Ripon, Yorkshire, which was presented to the people of Ripon by a Miss Cross to celebrate Queen Victoria's Diamond Jubilee. It was finished in 1897 but not officially opened until 1899. A Mr. King, who is still alive today, remembers a mulatto doing all the carvings. *Overleaf, right:* one of the many statues of Queen Victoria by Thomas Thorneycroft was placed on St. George's Plateau, Liverpool. Commissioned in 1869, it was completed two years later at a cost of £10,000.

By this time *The Builder* had been campaigning for years for more and better statues, monuments and memorials throughout the country. The campaign had been sparked off by Birmingham's poor and inglorious statue of Nelson, which was not only thought to be of poor quality but also to have been placed in totally inappropriate and pitifully barren surroundings. 'Only imagine', said *The Builder*, 'one statue to 200,000 living men.' In Rome or Athens there was one for every 100 or even 50 living men, but Birmingham, the great industrial city, could boast of only one, and an unappealing one at that. With the missing arm and the hollow sleeve, it was thought to be too literal and lifelike. Monumental statues should be an embodiment of the ideal, not an imitation of reality; the subject should be 'transfigured to the highest ideal of glory'. With these words *The Builder* opened its crusade.

Nelson was soon to come under fire again. On 3rd November 1843, when the great column was formally unveiled in Trafalgar Square, it was dismissed as being 'like a great stick or wand laid across a picture and always marring the view of it'. This had been a long, drawn-out project. The original competition for a design for the memorial was held in 1839, but the project was not completed until 1867, when the lions were finally put in position and the fountains and square laid out as we see them today. By this date heed must have been given to *The Builder's* fervent campaign, for it could now be claimed that 'London is unrivalled among the cities of Europe for its statues'.

Another popular embellishment of the street scene was the drinking fountain, and the Victorians built literally hundreds of them. In the late 1850s, a great campaign to erect drinking fountains swept over England, backed not only by the town planners but also by the forces of the temperance societies, who saw it as an opportunity to do something constructive with their money in their crusade against alcohol. Benjamin Scott, addressing a temperance meeting in the City of London, had this to say: 'There is one point of importance—that many of our citizens complain that they cannot find a wholesome substitute for beer or other drink; and I think the suggestion of having water fountains in London is a good one . . . I one day saw in Cornhill eight or ten people waiting at the pump there to drink; and it struck me that fountains or pumps in the streets would save men from drunkenness.'

The drinking fountain movement got under way and was heartily supported by *The Builder*: 'To those who doubt whether such a movement as this will tend to diminish drunkenness we would only say this—consider the fact that literally thousands quench their thirst in the course of a single day at only one of Liverpool's fountains; can any sceptic be so credulous as to believe that all these thousands, were there no such fountains, would carry their avowed thirst past the pot-house, and go home to tea or dinner as it

might be with blood as cool and free of alcohol as by the quenching of their thirst at the fountains?'

We must be grateful to all of the promoters of this cause, whatever their motives. Fountains appeared in every shape and size all over the country. No fancy whatever was curbed in their decoration, the only criterium being that they provided water, and hundreds of curious and elaborately decorated structures were made. Middleton-in-Teesdale, County Durham, can boast of one which has four crocodiles snapping at a baby sitting under an ornate arch. This, although so odd, might well have been a council design as it is to be found in two other villages nearby, though these are now wrecked almost beyond recognition. In Glasgow, under an immensely tall fountain topped by a stately Queen Victoria high up in the sky, superb bearded British Empire figures sit, life-size, in great arches. A fine figure in boots, representing Australia, with a kerchief and an open-necked shirt, is unexpectedly sitting next to an elegant woman in flowing robes holding sheaves of corn, her right hand resting on the head of a giant ram. India is represented by a turbaned Sikh with armour at his feet and a richly bejewelled lady by his side. In Stoke Row in Oxfordshire there is a magnificent Indian well, dating from 1863, which was given by the Maharajah of Benares. He had befriended the Lieutenant-Governor of the North-west provinces of India, a Mr. A. E. Reade, and the two had often spoken together of England. When Mr. Reade left India, as a mark of gratitude for his services, the Maharajah paid for this great well which the former Lieutenant-Governor, who was also an engineer, designed.

Fountains provided excellent excuses for decorative indulgence. *The Building News* reported in 1893 that one, heroic in scale, had just been completed in Cheltenham, representing Neptune and his attendants: 'Neptune appears with flowing hair seated on a chariot made of shell and drawn by seahorses. He is clothed in a mantle and holds in his hand a trident. On either side of him play sea-nymphs and tritons, their trumpets of shells. The entire structure is surrounded by balusters and at various points are vases filled with flowers.' At the opening ceremony the Mayor of Cheltenham explained that 'this work is part of a scheme for beautifying the Promenade', and that the long garden in front of the Promenade Terrace was about to be converted into an Italian garden, with ornamental railings and a bandstand in the centre.

Perfectionist as ever, giving attention to every detail, the Victorians even managed to encompass public conveniences into the integral design of their streets. Whether balustraded, embossed or gargoyled, these little cast-iron structures were every bit as pleasing as anything else in sight. Most were built in the middle of the nineteenth century. In 1850 there were only seventy-four in the whole of London, and it was felt that a concerted effort would have

35. *Opposite:* the Doulton fountain, made by the Doulton Glass Company for the International Exhibition in Glasgow in 1888. The designer was a Mr. Ayre.

AUSTRALIA

LET GLASGOW FLOURISH

to be made to improve the situation before the exhibition of 1851 opened. *The Builder* began another vigorous campaign for 'some plan by which the existing places may be made wholesome and not allowed to emit poisonous evaporations'. It went without saying, of course, that they would also have to be pleasing to the eye. There are a few which can still be seen, one in Reading, another at Great Ayton in Yorkshire, and another in Bristol. As little temples of convenience they were given their full due.

But then everything was given its full due, aesthetically, by the Victorians. And how very much more pleasing to the eye the street scene must have seemed then than it does today, with glimpses through ornate railings to ornate buildings beyond, approached through ornate gateways illuminated by ornate lamps. Admittedly, everything was elaborate and therefore not to everyone's taste. But the townscape was never oppressively of precisely the same style, and it was always put together with a gratifying sense of unity.

36. A Hindu well in Stoke Row, Oxfordshire, designed by A. E. Reade in 1863 and donated by the Maharajah of Benares.

Railway Stations

'Railway termini and hotels are to the nineteenth century what monasteries and cathedrals were to the thirteenth century. They are truly the only real representative buildings we possess.' So wrote *The Building News* in 1875. This parallel could equally well be drawn between the nineteenth-century smaller country station and the thirteenth-century parish church. The railway was nineteenth-century England's great triumph. Those iron rails, as well as supporting the Industrial Revolution, created an eruptive social revolution, bringing about changes of every kind and on every level wherever they went.

It was all on a grand scale. The face of the country was drastically altered by these 'iron veins'. A new society was created, new towns were born, new skills developed, new trades learnt and communications were improved to a startling degree; there was a new mobility, new prosperity, indeed a new life for many people. And, understandably, the Victorians saw fit to celebrate this affluence with the building of their splendid stations, temples as it were to the glory of such great achievements.

Frederick Smeeton Williams, in his excellent book *Our Iron Roads* (1852), wrote about 'the silent and gradual but mighty revolutions that have been effected in this country . . . by railways; augmenting in ever-increasing proportion and with ever-enlarging results, the intelligence, the wealth, and the welfare of the nation and the world.' To conclude this great volume the poet, Dr. Charles McKay, wrote:

> Lay down your rails, ye nations, near and far;
> Yoke your full trains to Steam's triumphal car; . . .
> Peace and improvement round each train shall soar,
> And knowledge light the ignorance of yore . . .
> Blessings on Science, and her handmaid, Steam!
> They make Utopia only half a dream . . .

A mania for the railway developed; there were special newspapers, the *Railway Times*, *Railway Express* and *Railway Standard*, all with engines steaming off amongst the letters. And a popular novel, *Earnest Struggles; or the Comic Incidents and Anxious Moments in Connection with The Life of a Station Master, by One who has Endured it*, was published. Its titillating associations with the railway were considered bound to make it a bestseller. There was a railway fever, and speculation took place on a massive scale. Bishops, bootboys and butlers, clerks and cowmen, and, according to Frederick Smeeton Williams, 'Peers and printers, vicars and vice-admirals, . . . gentlemen's cooks and Queen's Counsels . . . with a multitude of other callings unrecorded in the Book of Trades' all indulged in the excitement of share buying, and it was respectable to do so. 'Bland country vicars became "bears", curates were "stags", and old maiden ladies became "bulls" in the Stock Exchange.'

Rivalry between the railway companies, too, was determined and often foolish. Lines were even sent off in quite unsuitable directions simply to forestall others. In 1835 *John Bull* denounced it all as 'destructive of the country in a thousand particulars—the whole face of the kingdom to be tattooed with these odious deformities—huge mounds are to intersect our beautiful valleys; the noise and stench of locomotive steam engines are to disturb the quietude of the peasant, the farmer and the gentleman; and the roaring of the bullocks, the bleating of the sheep and the grunting of the pigs to keep up one continual roar through the night along the lines of these most dangerous and disfiguring abominations.'

Enemies of the railway there were. A cartoon by George Cruikshank shows a scene of typically imagined terror, 'The Railway Dragon, A Nightmare', illustrating the fears of hundreds. A great beast of an engine is backing into a family's dining room. With fiery eyes and boiler aflame for a mouth, it devours whole sides of beef and whole round Christmas puddings, while the mother stands by screaming, 'Oh my beef! oh my babies!' 'I come to dine, I come to sup, I come, I come . . . to eat you up!' chants the engine. The railway was considered by some to be a fearsome intrusion, bringing the threat of industrialization to the lives of everyone. 'Our Merrie England', wrote Ruskin, 'has changed into the "Man with the Iron Mask".' But the railways were not built for the spiritual uplift of the aesthetic movement. Ruskin felt 'transmuted' into a 'living parcel' when on a train. Their effect, however, was far greater than any that he could ever have hoped to aspire to.

By 1845 some 12,936,927 people, equal to half the population of England at the time, had travelled on the railways. This new and useful mobility was not limited to people. By 1846 Williams calculated that if all the animals that had travelled had been 'marshalled in procession ten abreast and 10 feet apart, the line of horses would extend for 6 miles; the phalanx of pigs would be 44 miles in length; there would be 9 miles of dogs, 60 miles of cattle, and 160 miles of sheep. In other words, there would be a procession of horses, pigs, dogs, cattle, and sheep ten abreast, extending so far

7. The beautiful deep platform canopy, under which there are ɔose boxes for people to sit in, at Hanwell Station, Ealing, London. This was an early Great Western tation, and therefore probably ates from the 1840s. Despite the act that it has been listed for four ears, British Rail have made no ffort to retain this station. According to the Hanwell Preservation Society, who are onstantly pressing for something o be done, they are in fact slowly emolishing it, instead of making epairs. The shelter on the outh-bound platform is now only ɔartially standing and that line as been closed. The fire buckets hat used to hang in a row have all ɔone, as has the station sign on he central platform and the south ide of the central platform 'alance. On 22nd March 1975 the ɡas lights were replaced by stark, ɔare electric bulbs on wires, ɔanging inelegantly between the ɔld gas globes.

that, while the near ranks of sheep were bleating in London, the front ranks of the horses would be neighing among the hills of Cumberland.'

Farmers in the early days had prophesied nothing less than the ruination of their land (by the late 1840s, the value of farming land had risen by ten shillings an acre) and terror to their animals. Unless hoardings were put up between the lines and the fields (according to Cyril Bruyn Andrews in *The Railway Age*, 1937), it was said that the cows' milk would be sure to dry up. The working lives of horses, too, were obviously under serious threat. 'No more panting flanks and furrowed ribs, no drooping heads and blood red nostrils . . . only ribs of steel, bowels of brass and breath of steam.' The steam horse was bound to conquer.

They were all of them 'mares: those little iron horses', according to a certain Miss Fanny Kemble. In a letter dated 20th April 1830, she wrote, in praise of railways, that: 'a common sheet of paper is enough for love, but a foolscap extra alone can contain a railroad and my ecstasies'. Of the great George Stephenson (1781–1848) she said: 'his face is fine, though careworn, and bears an expression of deep thoughtfulness; his mode of explaining his ideas is peculiar and very original, striking, and forcible; and, although his accent indicates strongly his north-country birth, his language has not the slightest touch of vulgarity or coarseness.' By this time Stephenson was a figure of considerable importance. Almost single-handed he had put the railway on to its tracks and by 1830 had achieved enormous technological feats with the building of both the Stockton and Darlington and the Liverpool and Manchester lines, respectively the first and second in the world to carry passengers.

The son of a collier, Stephenson was born in the village of Wylam, County Durham, and when still a small child was earning two pence a day picking 'bats and dross' from the coal heaps. As a young man, he was employed as an engine stoker by Lord Ravensworth, who, by increasing his wages in 1800 from one shilling to a princely two shillings a day, caused Stephenson to alter his plans to emigrate to America and so secured for England its splendid railway beginnings and prosperity. In 1825, under the same patronage, the first public railway in the world, the Stockton and Darlington, was opened, with Stephenson as the appointed engineer and surveyor. After nine years of persuasion and three defeats in Parliament, he and Edward Pease, who in dealing with the financial side of the project had only managed to sell twenty shares, had succeeded at last. But there was still opposition: 'I am sorry to find', said Lord Eldon, 'the intelligent people of the north

38. Ticket booth of the first railway station in the world—Liverpool Road, Manchester, which was opened in September 1830 by the Duke of Wellington. The stationmaster's house and the ticket office alone remain intact, and even they are in a sorry state of repair.

country gone mad on the subject of railways.' Even purely for the transportation of coal their value was not widely recognized: 'It is all very well to spend money', said a representative of a local authority, 'if it will do some good, but I will eat all the coal that your railroad will carry.' 'He did not live', said Pease's son Henry, 'until the year 1874, when 127,000,000 tons of coal were carried by the railway, and I hope that he had many good dinners on much more digestable material.'

In 1826, 500 acres of land a few miles from Stockton were bought by the Railway Company to deal with the new influx of traffic—one solitary farmhouse in the midst of green fields was transformed into Middlesbrough, by 1883 a town of some 50,000 inhabitants, with its origins solely due to the railway. In this way the face of England was changed. New towns sprung up, others were enlarged beyond recognition, while those neglected by the railways faded away. Crewe was a creation of the railways and again originated from a single farmhouse. *The Builder* of 1846 records the plans and aspirations for the new town: The 'villa style' was recommended for 'superior officers'. A kind of 'ornamental Gothic' was thought suitable for 'the next in authority', while the engineers were domiciled in 'detached mansions which accommodate four families'. '. . . the labourer delights in neat cottages of four apartments, the entrances within ancient porches; all have gardens, and, to the credit of the labourers, one of them, in a recent floral show, carried away the prize.' Two clergymen were provided, one Church of England and the other Church of Scotland, and there were playgrounds, a newsroom, schools, an assembly room and baths—one penny each 'when they use it'.

Swindon was another such town. In 1838, according to Williams, 'a little party of gentlemen sat down on the greensward to take their luncheon. "The furze was in blossom around them; the rabbits frisked in and out of their burrows; two or three distant farmhouses, one or two cottages, these were all the signs of human habitation, except a few cart-ruts, indicating a track used for field purposes".' These gentlemen, among them Isambard Kingdom Brunel, were sitting where one of Swindon Station's platforms stands today, in the heart of that vast railway town. The landscape of England was drastically altering. 'At every other mile', wrote George Eliot, 'some sign of worldwide change, some new direction of human labour, has brought itself into what one may call the speech of the landscape. There comes a crowd of burly navvies with pickaxes and barrows and, while hardly a wrinkle is made in the fading mother's face or a new curve of health in the blooming girl's, the hills are cut through, or the breeches between them spanned.'

This swarm of encroaching navvies was a terrible intrusion on the peace of the countryside. They themselves, with their burly

39-41. Central ceiling pendant, from which would have hung a gasolier, (*opposite, top*) and one of the eight elaborate ceiling bosses (*opposite, bottom*) in the royal waiting-room at Windsor, Eton and Riverside Station (see also Pl. XVII). The ceiling bosses decorate the intersections of the panelled ceiling with tudor roses, poppies and thistles. The station was designed in 1851 by Sir William Tite and is now part of the offices of a firm of architects. *Above:* decorated lavatory flues and the wooden valance over the entrance to Cheddar Station, Somerset, 1869. The platform canopy here, which was demolished in the 1960s, was designed by Brunel. British Rail claim that this sadly decaying building is being restored, but Industrial Mailing and Marketing Ltd., who now use it as offices, say that only their presence is keeping it standing and that the entrance valance alone has been restored.

roughness, were bad enough, but what they were hewing the land asunder for was considered an abomination, a thundering threat to rural existence, and vicars and landlords stood fast. Surveyors could do their evil clandestine work only when the clergymen were safely in their pulpits. According to Andrews, a certain 'reverend gentleman' complained that his family's privacy had been ruined, because his daughter's windows faced on to the 'unhallowed gaze' of the navigators. He demanded, and received, considerable compensation, saying that he and his family would be obliged to recover at a watering place, and that a new curate would have to be engaged! All was paid, but the family never moved. 'The unhappy family have still dwelt in their desecrated abode, and borne with Christian-like resignation all the miseries heaped upon them. The gilding of the pill, it seems, has rendered it palatable, and we have no doubt that if his daughter's room has a back window as well as a front one, he would be exceedingly glad if a railroad was carried across that at the same price.' The clergy were always being made fun of. The Manchester and Southampton Railways were said to be fit only for 'parsons and prawns' and a detailed account of a rather serious accident at Croydon describes how 'a right reverend prelate suffered from an unfortunate collision of his nose'.

The landed gentry's supremacy, too, was at risk; the combination of the unified mass of the working people with their symbol of newly-acquired power must have seemed highly disagreeable. Massive compensations were paid when the lands of the nobility were invaded. The Duke of Bedford, to his great credit, returned his full £150,000 on the grounds that his estate had in fact benefited. Splendid bathing and fishing pavilions were built for Lord Cloncurry by the Dublin and Kingston Railway in compensation for its passing through his estate, but other landowners bestowed approval and some had stations especially built for them. Pugin himself is said to have designed Alton to serve Alton Towers, the Duke of Shrewsbury's great house, and Sir Charles Barry built Trentham for the Duke of Sutherland's Trentham Hall. The Duke of Rutland had the most splendid private waiting-room at Redmile, with a vast oak chimneypiece richly carved up to the ceiling—it framed a scene in stone of the hunt in full cry, with Belvoir Castle in the background. Naked caryatids supported it from the floor.

A number of great architects involved themselves in the designing of stations. Sir William Tite built the one at Barnes, on the London and South Western line, a charming little multi-gabled, high-chimneyed country station, and that at Windsor, Eton and

42, 43. *Above left:* Manchester Central Station, 1876–9, by Sir John Fowler. The vast platform canopy has a single span of 210 feet. This derelict station is now in the hands of private developers. There has been talk of retaining the main cast-iron shed (which is listed Grade Two) as an exhibition centre, but the rest of the 23-acre site, which contains many fine railway warehouses, is to be redeveloped to provide offices and city roads. *Above right:* detail of one of the windows, all of which are diamond paned, of Wateringbury Station, Kent, 1844 (see also Pl. XVI). A third of this station has now been demolished.

44, 45. *Above and right:* Richmond Station, Yorkshire, 1847. Designed by G. T. Andrews, architect of the original York Station, it was closed in 1869 as it was running at a loss. The building was repaired by the district council in 1973–4 and has been let to a local businessman as a garden centre.

46. *Above:* arched stained-glass window
and doorway on a platform at Great
Malvern Station, Worcestershire. This
was designed in 1859 by E. W. Elmslie.
In the foreground is one of the naturalistic cast-iron capitals (see Pl. XIX).

47, 48. St. Pancras Station, London.
Designed by Sir George Gilbert Scott,
the building was completed in 1869.
Right: one of several Gothic ticket
booths. These are joined to each other
by elaborate panelling. *Far right:*
decorative corbel in the booking office.
There are four of these, on which an
engine driver, an engineer, a signalboy,
and, on this one, a guard, are sculpted.

Riverside, an ornate gem, whose waiting-room was designed especially for Queen Victoria. But with Gosport Station, the exquisite terminus of the London and Southampton line, he had his greatest triumph of all. The beautiful fourteen-bay Tuscan colonnade now stands sadly neglected, surrounded by the growth of nature within and Gosport without.

Other architects' names were made by their achievements in railway architecture alone. For example, Francis Thompson produced a set of buildings of the highest quality for the North Midland Railway, and indeed that great arbiter of taste, John Claudius Loudon turned architectural ideals a full circle with a set of villas based on Thompson's station designs. George Townshend Andrews was another figure of note, who enriched the landscape of Yorkshire with his excellent use of local materials when building his stations. It seems to have been understood, indeed, that the essence of a really good country station was that it should blend into its surrounding countryside and, in some cases with the company's architect or engineer in charge, in others with an architect of importance, they all by and large succeeded in doing this superbly well.

Cheddar Station, a charming example, now in a sad state of decay, fits into the landscape neatly and beautifully and, indeed,

its presence actually enhances the spot. With its cream-coloured stone walls and bargeboarding, scalloped tiled roof and finely decorated flues, the colours and shapes give no suggestion of a foreign intruder. The station at Wateringbury in Kent was converted from a country house: built in red brick, with diamond-shaped leaded light windows, it sits happily by the riverside looking for all the world as if it is still a home and a part of rural life. And that at Richmond in Yorkshire, by Andrews, in dour grey stone Gothic in deference to the castle nearby, fits perfectly into the townscape and in no way represents the intrusive industrialization that it might have done.

The photographs of these country and smaller town stations have not in fact been chosen for this quality of blending into the landscape alone, but rather for the special and curious feeling of railway architecture that they all have in common. Embellishment was sometimes on a riotous scale, sometimes hardly in evidence at all, but there is some indefinable quality that runs through all of the stations. They were after all the inventions of the Victorians, and such an architectural adventure is bound to have produced characteristic results.

Enormous trouble was involved in their design. 'As an architectural thesis', said *The Building News* in 1877, '. . . it was a crucial one . . . requiring more than ordinary effort in its accomplishment.' It was describing a competition for the design of a small railway station for which an elaborate and curious selection of entries had been submitted by competitors all using pseudonyms. 'Johnny Orange Blossom' produced a 'free kind of Gothic', 'Noah's' was 'of Queen Anne character', while 'Cave Canem' entered 'Early Gothic with narrow pointed lights and transoms', and 'St. Lucy' 'a design resembling more a village school than a Railway Station'. 'Tempus Fugit's' design was fragile and fussy, and so on. It was a very serious business. 'Magnet' was advised to try again—'alas for corpulent people when they pass through such narrow doorways!'

Many stations were extravagantly fine. Great Malvern in Worcestershire is one of the most splendid of all, twenty-eight pillars march up the platforms, fourteen a side, with exquisitely wrought-iron capitals decorated with conkers, lilies, and strawberries, all superbly lifelike in their newly repainted, original clear and strong colours. Tynemouth in Northumberland was a forest of intricate ironwork; one was engulfed in its finery the moment one entered the station. It can no longer be seen but, thankfully, it has not been demolished, but was bricked-in two days after the photograph was taken in 1972.

British Rail does seem to be far too unconcerned with the fate of this fascinating architectural heritage that it holds in its hands. It quite fairly claims that it is wrong to spend the

49. *Opposite:* elaborately bargeboarded footbridge at Taplow Station, Buckinghamshire, 1872. There was a line through Taplow from 1838 but no station for thirty-four years. The station buildings are bright red brick with white arches and facings.

50. *Overleaf:* Tynemouth Station, Northumberland, 1882, attributed to William Bell, architect of the North Eastern Railway.

taxpayer's money, given to it to run trains, on architectural restoration, but it seems a very great pity that some kind of serious conservationist policy cannot be worked out. Euston Station Arch—'Key to the gateways of London'—the magnificent Doric propylaeum by Philip Hardwick, whose pillars alone were 44 feet high, was built to commemorate the glory of the railways in 1837. The scandal of its demolition in 1965 is well known and, in 1975, it looks as if there might be another one: Liverpool Street Station, with its cathedral-like depth of arches and pillars is threatened—23 acres are to be cleared to make way for 1·25 million square feet of offices. Ambergate Station in Derbyshire, built by Francis Thompson for the North Midland Railway, where Stephenson was engineer, was in 1840 a delightful melody of shapes: Dutch gabling, tall elaborate chimneys, stone balls and balustrades. In 1971, it was a trail of rubble on either side of two smashed platforms. The station at Melton Mowbray in Leicestershire has ended up, in part, at a nearby home, fashioned into 'natural stone' fireplaces, while that at Aldermaston was knocked down by mistake in the early 1970s. If for no other reason, they are interesting as architectural examples of buildings which have never changed their function since they were built, but they also epitomize the architecture of the Victorians, reflecting all their spirit with the multitude of styles they so enjoyed building in.

Ruskin hated the whole business: 'Better bury gold in the embankments, than put it in ornaments on the stations . . . Will a single traveller be willing to pay an increased fare on the South Western, because the columns of the terminus are covered with patterns from Nineveh? . . . you would not put rings on the fingers of a smith at his anvil.'

But embellishment is not the only thing that makes the architecture of nineteenth-century railway stations unique: it is that indefinable but immediately recognizable quality that runs through them all that is so pleasing. They were created with pride in the knowledge that in these buildings the designers led the world; and today this pride still shines through every one of the Victorian railway stations still standing.

XX. *Opposite:* the stone lion tomb of George Wombell, menagerist, in Highgate Cemetery, Swain's Lane London N.6. Dating from 1887, this is one of the few figurative tombs in this cemetery, which contains mainly only urns and obelisks. Highgate was laid out in 1838–9 by Stephen Geary, who is also reputed to have designed the first gin palace in London. It is now closed to the public due to vandalism.

TO THE MEMORY
OF
GEORGE WOMBWELL.
(MENAGERIST)
BORN 24TH DECR 1777.
DIED 16TH NOVR 1850.

XXI, XXII. Kensal Green Cemetery, London W.10 (see also Pls. 52 and 56). *Above:* a stone baby and pony on a shelf-tomb, inscribed 'To the Memory of the beloved wife of William Cooke who departed this life at Bognor, August 6th 1874, aged 65 years.' *Below:* vast canopied monument, 'Sacred to the Memory of Major-General the Hon. Sir William Casement, K.C.B., of the Bengal Army and member of the Supreme Council of India,' who, after forty-seven and a half years, deferred his departure from India, 'a step which exposed him to the attack of the fatal malady which terminated his valuable life at Cossipore on the . . . day of April 1844, in the 64th year of his age. . . .'

XXIII. *Opposite:* detail of the sandstone tomb, in a graveyard in Coughton, Warwickshire, of schoolboy Edward Jackson, who died on 25th August 1851, aged fifteen. 'My boy, my boy, thy father calls in vain . . . not hear his once lov'd voice again. . . .' His pony, with a cast-iron mortar board on the saddle, and also his gun, cricket bats, fishing rod and creel are carved in sandstone.

XXIV. *Above:* the grave, in a
churchyard in Offton, Suffolk, of John
Wyard, who collapsed and died in a
stable on 7th January 1867. His sister
and his horse watch over the covered
corpse.

XXV, XXVI. *Left:* detail of the tiled
and pillared entrance hall in the Royal
Courts of Justice Restaurant, 222
Strand, London W.C.2. Dating from
1883, it was taken over by Lloyds Bank
in 1895 after both the first and the
second 'Palsgrave Restaurant' eating-
house ventures had failed. It has a
highly decorated interior with Doulton
tiles on the walls. *Opposite:* detail of a
stained-glass window in the Oyster Bar
of the Café Royal, Edinburgh (see also
Pl. 70). The windows, depicting life-size
sportsmen, were designed by a Mr.
Wilson in 1890–1900 for J. Ballantyre &
Sons, stained-glass artists who also did
work in the House of Lords in London.

XXIX, XXX. The Tottenham, Oxford Street, London W.1., designed in 1890 by architects Saville and Martin. The interior decoration has been retained and even restored. There is a frieze of tiles, some of which have been broken, and the brewery, unable to replace them with ceramics, have had the same pattern painted in. *Above:* detail of one of the richly painted mirrors, all of which are framed in mahogany. *Below:* detail of a fake tapestry, which is made up of oil paints on tapestry weave. A series of these alternate with the painted mirrors, which are the same size, along the full length of the wall.

XXVII, XXVIII, XXXI. The Philharmonic, Hope Street, Liverpool, 1898–1900, by Walter Thomas. Artists and designers from the University School of Art contributed their specialist crafts under the direction of Paul Neil and Arthur Stratten. Ships' carpenters were responsible for the joinery. *Opposite, top:* the saloon bar, with plasterwork by sculptor Charles Allen. *Opposite, bottom:* the gentlemen's lavatory, with marble urinal stalls and cistern. The marble washbasin is supported by cast-iron angels. *Overleaf:* the public bar, with its sweep of mosaic and mahogany. Beaten copper panels by H. Blomfield Barr are let into the mahogany wall panelling.

XXXII. *Above:* the private bar of the Vines, Lime Street, Liverpool, showing the beaten copper and painted plaster picture over the fireplace, and the heavy plaster frieze which continues all round the room. The Vines was built in 1898–1900 by Walter Thomas (see also Pls. 58, 59).

XXXIII-XXXV. The Great Eastern Hotel, on the corner of Bishopsgate and Liverpool Street, London E.C.2. *Left:* the Grecian temple, with its 'exceedingly handsome chairs' and where 'great use was made of Breche marble', according to a contemporary brochure (see also Pl. 68). *Opposite, top:* a mural of the ark in the Egyptian temple. This is one of the paintings that go right round the room at frieze level. *Opposite, bottom:* the organ and the tapered Egyptian doorway in the Egyptian temple. Two great pillars support the ceiling at each end.

XXXVI. *Overleaf:* Cottars Howff, 21 Rose Street, Edinburgh. Enormous stained-glass window, in three sections, showing a Black Watch soldier dying in the Crimean War. The side panels give the names of the battles in which the regiment fought.

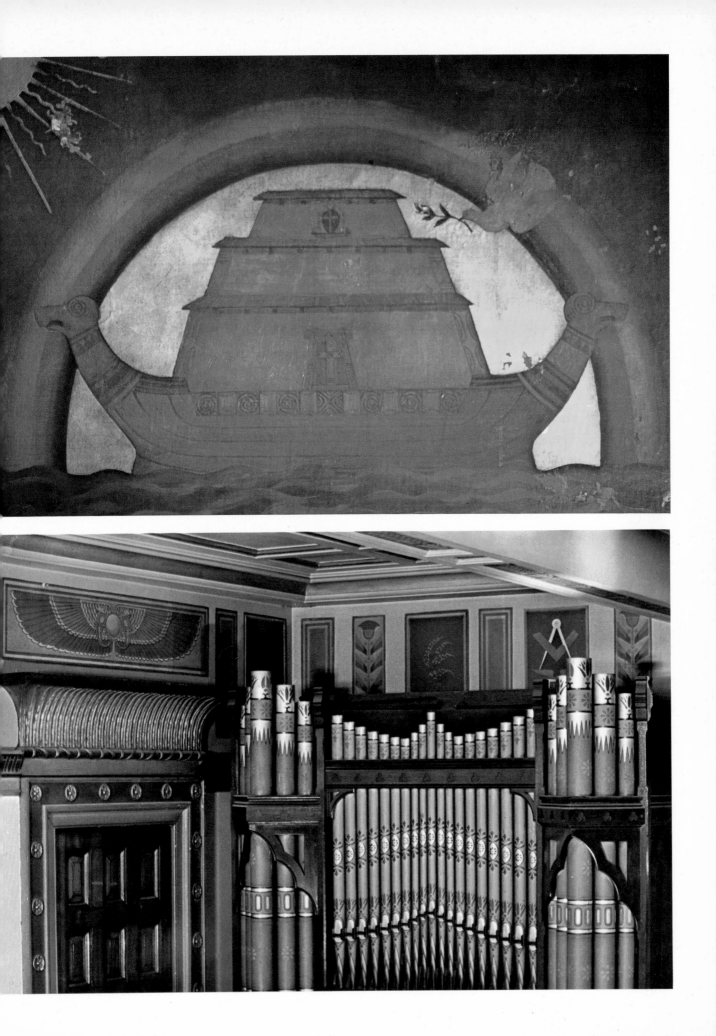

XXXVIII, XXXIX. *Above:* façade of a butcher's shop in Mount Street, London W.1. This was built as part of the large terracotta development there in the late 1890s. *Below right:* early 1900s tiled exterior of Crofts, general hardware store, 46 Heath Road, Twickenham, London. Inside there are still the uncovered boards on the floor, and behind the wooden counter the whole wall is covered with a mass of minute brass-handled compartments.

XXXVII. *Opposite:* tiled mural, by W. J. Neatby, of split stylized tree trunks in the meat hall of Harrods, Knightsbridge, London (see also Pl. 76).

Graves

A Victorian figure, Mr. Earl Drax, used regularly to rehearse his own funeral. Sitting up in an open coffin being patiently borne by a procession of gamekeepers and gardeners, he would shout his orders: 'Hi! Down with your eyes. Keep in step—you're shaking the corpse'. He had an immense mausoleum built for himself at Holnest in Dorset which was demolished in 1923–4.

This is an extravagant example of the Victorian attitude to death—but extravagant really only in its degree of eccentricity. The Victorians were obsessed by death. They were bound to be. With tragedy (death) an everyday possibility rather than an ultimate fate, indulgence in the elaborate, in the ceremonial, in rich sentiment and melancholy must have provided some defence, or at least a buffer, against such constant and raw grief. And indulge in it they did, wholeheartedly, almost celebrating the event of death. Durham miners were known to be propped up at the head of the table and toasted at their own funeral feasts, presiding for the last time over their households as their families gobbled the funeral fare.

The pictures that accompany this chapter only deal with one aspect of death and the Victorians—their graves, headstones, sepulchral monuments and mausoleums; but something must be said about the extraordinary atmosphere that led to the construction of such exquisite memorials to the dead.

There were many other reasons as to why this absorbing interest in death was on such a massive scale. Religion was being threatened by science, and to protect it the Victorians wallowed even deeper in sentiment. The new middle classes, now well able to afford to honour their dead, did so with relish, displaying their wealth and substance with highly perfected mourning etiquette and with vast funerals, finally sending their families off to eternal respectability under their noble tombs and monuments.

The death of so many children, too, must have enhanced the sentimental side of their grief.

> Why did Baby die,
> Making Father cry,
> Mother cry?
>
> Flowers that bloom to die,
> Make no reply
> Of 'Why'?
> But bow and die.

XL. *Opposite:* James Smith and Sons (Umbrellas) Ltd., 53 New Oxford Street, London W.C.1. (see also Pl. 83). Dating from 1857, the façade of this corner site still remains intact.

This poem by Christina Rosetti is typical of many hundreds. It is illustrated by a tiny cross and a mound being wept over by two embracing elder children.

In Keighley, Yorkshire, a certain Rebecca Town died in 1851 aged forty-four years, having had thirty children, only one of whom survived to the age of three. In Easton in Gordano, Somerset, Harriet Pains lies together with her fourteen brothers and sisters, all of whom died in infancy, she herself dying at the age of ten. This was not unusual, for the infant mortality rate in the nineteenth century was horrifying. Up until the twentieth century, roughly a hundred and fifty out of every thousand babies born alive died in infancy, and older children were so vulnerable to the killers—cholera and consumption—that they were likewise viciously struck down. Thousands died: 'The pale, consumption was the final blow, the stroke was fatal, the effect came slow'.

John Morley, in his book *Death, Heaven and the Victorians* (1971), tells us that in Manchester alone, in 1840, more than fifty-seven out of every hundred working-class children were dead before reaching the age of five. In *Victorian Cities* (1963), Asa Briggs recounts that, in the years 1871–3, in Middlesbrough, forty per cent of the deaths recorded were of infants under the age of one year, with children between the ages of one and five years account-

51. This used to be one of the few graves that remained intact in the now overgrown Nunhead Cemetery at Peckham, London S.E.15., which was laid out by James Bunstone Bunning in the early 1840s for the London Cemetery Company. However, since the photograph was taken, this grave of John Allen, who was born in Yorkshire on 8th August 1790 and died on 29th May 1805, has been smashed.

ing for a further twenty per cent. Cholera, 'the pestilence that walketh in the darkness', with its alarming secret funerals crashing through the night, although certainly striking harder at the overcrowded slum areas, carried away many people in the more protected classes as well.

With the coming of the Industrial Revolution, overcrowding in towns grew to terrifying proportions, and the dark, dank burial grounds of the cities became quite unable to deal with the staggering death rate. Rotting corpses were disinterred to make way for others, which in their turn, perhaps as soon as a week later, would be gouged up to make room for yet more. As early as the 1820s, several London churchyards were reported to have upwards of 3000 corpses per acre. Pulled up from their graves, chopped up with axes and saws especially kept for the purpose, they would be thrown into the carnel- or bone-houses and left to rot, sometimes even to be sold for manure.

In 1843 some 50,000 corpses were stacked into the 150 graveyards of London, and the consequences were devilish. With putrid and poisonous gases issuing from these pits and the air 'dark with vapours', something had to be done. According to Sir Walter Besant, in *London in the Nineteenth Century* (1909), a Dr. Walker, who published numerous pamphlets agitating against the dangers and scandals of burial grounds, thus described St. Sepulchre, Snow Hill:

> With a population including Middlesex of 13,500, it has two 'slips' on either side of the church, which together can if at all exceed a quarter of an acre. There are vaults under the church; but if anyone, having perceived the effluvia some yards from the open door, can descend, unimpelled by duty or private feeling, he has stronger nerves than the writer's, although sorely taxed in this troublesome world.

France led the way to reform, with the romantic necropolis of Père Lachaise in Paris; Glasgow, Belfast and Liverpool followed, and the glorious tide of cemeteries began to sweep over the land—stately, spacious landscaped parks wherein the dead could repose at last in uninterrupted peace. Many of these great cemeteries, grandiose showpieces of their time, are now in a serious state of neglect, and soon it will be too late to untangle them from the roots, weeds and rubble that are slowly enveloping these vast tracts of land.

Nunhead, a cemetery of some 50 acres in a particularly dismal part of South London, is an oasis of wilderness where foxes and badgers run free. Almost every nineteenth-century gravestone has been smashed, and many prised open, leaving piles of rubble. The grass is waist high, the chapel falling down and the two lodges already in ruins. It was laid out in the early 1840s by James

Bunstone Bunning, the architect of the great London Coal Exchange, after the usual competition to decide who should undertake what was considered to be a most important work. John Claudius Loudon, in his *On the laying out, planting, and managing of cemeteries; and on the improvement of churchyards*, written in 1843, says that a most important point to be noted 'is the influence which a cemetery or churchyard is calculated to have in improving the taste of the people', and further suggests that:

> a church and churchyard in the country, or general cemetery . . . properly designed, laid out, ornamented with tombs, planted with trees, shrubs, and herbaceous plants, all named, and the whole properly kept, might become a school of instruction in architecture, sculpture, landscape gardening or arboriculture, botany, and in those important parts of general gardening, neatness, order and high keeping.

Nunhead is an extreme case of neglect, but others are all too swiftly following the same path. Highgate possesses few graves intact in its rampaging wilderness, with vandalism reaching the repulsive point of human excreta on Radclyffe Hall's tomb. Norwood is seemingly safe and is crammed with fine monuments. A glowing red-brick mausoleum to the Doulton family is well worth

52. A general view of Kensal Green Cemetery, London W.10., showing how beautiful a reasonably maintained nineteenth-century cemetery can be (see also Pls. XXI, XXII, 56). The undergrowth is kept under control and the landscaped tombs and trees create enchanting vistas. Unfortunately, however, massive modern black and white marble slabs are starting to appear amongst the old monuments. The cemetery was laid out in 1832 by the General Cemetery Company and achieved permanent respectability by the burial there of Princess Sophia, daughter of George III. Also buried there are Isambard Kingdom Brunel, Wilkie Collins, Anthony Trollope, Leigh Hunt and William Makepeace Thackeray.

seeing there, as is another nearby, in crumbling stone and bright ceramic; sadly its inscription is illegible, and so it is not known whom it commemorates. An interesting Greek cemetery within this one, bought by the brotherhood of the Greek community in 1842, lies at the north-east corner. Crowded with great tombs, there is one mausoleum to the Ralli family which was designed by no less a personage than G. E. Street, the architect of the London Law Courts. Mrs. Beaton and Sir William Cubitt are also buried at Norwood.

Kensal Green was the first great nineteenth-century cemetery to be built in London. Primrose Hill had been considered, but finally 54 acres of land were bought, for the sum of £9,400, just off the Harrow Road in what was then a completely rural area. A great plantation of trees was planned, with 800 being planted immediately, and a competition was held for the design of a chapel with vaults and a gatehouse with lodges. According to James Stevens Curl, in his book *The Victorian Celebration of Death* (1972), many 'proposed picturesque arrangements' were submitted, and the 'battle of the Styles', Classical versus Gothic, raged complete within this small issue alone. The classicists won, and the heavy Doric chapel and gatehouse by Chadwick that we see today was built rather than the charming Gothic chapel, watergate and gatehouse designed by H. E. Kendall. In Kensal Green, the Victorians' finest hopes and aspirations for their cemeteries came true: the tombs are magnificent, the landscaping, although in places overgrown, is soothing and spacious, and it is indeed, as it was meant to be, 'a morally uplifting' place to visit, reflecting the tastes, dreams and ideals of the age.

The glorious hope of eternal peace, rather than the indecency of the charnel-house, was now a reality, adding a little more fuel to the already fiercely burning flames of sentimentality. It was also another justification for having such splendid funerals to see the dead off to their now properly final places of rest. These funerals were astonishing, involving colossal costs—sometimes as much as £1,000 for the procession alone, and on top of that a grand mausoleum could cost up to £3,000 more. Woe betide you if you could not afford some sort of display. Dead children were sometimes abandoned in the street so that the family would not have to face the shame of a parish funeral, and corpses could be kept in the house for as long as two weeks while the money for the ceremony was scraped together.

Your funeral established or betrayed your social position. Burial clubs were formed into which money was paid weekly to ensure a decent burial. Many such clubs being dishonest, people enrolled in more than one, and grim tales emerged of children being allowed to die, the radiant haul from the club being too much to resist. Mourning after a death was stifling and severe: for a widow, a rigorous and unrelieved display of grief had to be kept up for as long as two-and-a-half years; six months was expected when your child had died, and the second wife was obliged to mourn the death of the first wife's parents for six weeks!

The example of the Queen, 'The Widow of Windsor', must have helped to convince the people of the necessity and respectability of such etiquette. She kept her ladies of the court in mourning for a full forty years after Prince Albert's death, allowing them only to wear black, white, grey or mauve. Albert's picture, entwined in a memorial wreath, hung above the empty pillow beside her every night of her life, and in death they lie together at Frogmore, below two life-size statues which were commissioned by her in 1862. They appear both young and asleep, she with her head slightly inclined towards him.

Sculpture, an offshoot of the obsession with death, found in the grandest cemetery as well as in the smallest country churchyard, is a rich and curious heritage for us to feast our eyes upon today. From Major-General the Hon. Sir William Casement's vast canopy supported by four 12-foot-high caryatids, at Kensal Green, to the astonishing, lace-clad porcelain baby at Courteen Hall, Northamptonshire, whose bonnet is so exquisitely wrought, with each threaded ribbon, tuck and fold included; or to the carved spurs, whip,

53. Top of the tombstone in Brockenhurst, Hampshire, of Harry 'Brusher' Mills, so-called because he used to brush the New Forest cricket ground, 'and for a number of years followed the occupation of snake catcher in the New Forest'. His pursuit and the primitive way in which he lived caused him to be an object of interest to many. According to a man who knew him, he drank a bottle of brandy a day, never washed, and had 'an aroma all of his own'. He died in 1905.

fox's mask and saddle in memory of an old huntsman of Bilsdale, the sculptors' artistry and originality are remarkable. They worked in Portland stone, slate, pink and yellow sandstone, Cotswold stone and whatever local stone was handy at the time.

Part of the landscape and life of the land, the country church had been for centuries an integral part of village life, a shared concern and responsibility for the people, helping them through life and sheltering them in death. In their churchyards local people are recorded with affection: blacksmiths, watchmakers, auctioneers, engine drivers, policemen, shepherds, fishwives, gamekeepers, gardeners—all are remembered for their individuality. There is even a snake catcher recorded at Brockenhurst in Hampshire.

In Bromsgrove, Worcestershire, there are two gravestones with oval panels bearing low-relief carvings of steam engines. They commemorate Thomas Scaife and Joseph Rutherford, engineers of the Birmingham and Gloucester Railways. Scaife was killed on Tuesday 10th November 1840, when an engine boiler exploded at Bromsgrove station. Rutherford died a day later, presumably as a result of the same accident. The gravestones are painted black and white, as their original dark red stone makes it difficult to see the details, and that of Joseph Rutherford bears the following inscription:

> My engine now is cold and still,
> No water does my boiler fill,
> My coke affords it flames no more,
> My days of usefulness are o'er.
> My wheels deny their noted speed
> No more my guiding hands they heed.
> My whistle too has lost its tone
> Its shrill and thrilling sounds are gone
> My valves are now thrown open wide
> My flanges all refuse to guide
> My clacks, also, though once too strong
> Refuse to aid the busy throng
> No more I feel each urging breath
> My steam is now condens'd in death
> Life's railway o'er, each station's past
> In death I'm stopped, and rest at last.
> Farewell dear friends and cease to weep
> In Christ I'm safe, in him I sleep.

How much more revealing this epitaph is than the impersonal black and white marble slabs lined up in churchyards and cemeteries today.

They were great craftsmen, these nineteenth-century stonemasons. Following the same trade as generations of their families before them, they produced vigorously original work and carved

all manner of curiosities into the English churchyard. A beehive for a gardener in Greenford, Middlesex; a helmet, truncheon, belt and lamp for a policeman in Montgomery, Wales; a 12-foot-high model of a railway tunnel for the twenty-eight men killed while constructing it, at Otley, Yorkshire; cricket stumps for cricketers both at Lewknor in Oxfordshire and Sawston in Cambridgeshire; a pink sandstone pony with a cast-iron mortar board on its saddle for a schoolboy in Coughton, Warwickshire; an organ for the wife of an organ maker at Kildwick in Yorkshire; an anchor in South-wold, Suffolk, a lion at Highgate, London—right into the grandest city cemeteries this more modest branch of masonry flourished. Close to the gigantic mausoleums and monuments at Kensal Green is the delightful sight of a small stone girl in an exquisite lace dress and high button boots; near to her sits a whippet on a cushion, mourning his mistress.

Town and country alike were engulfed in this sweeping tide of grief: there was a fascination with death. *Crabtree Fold*, a woe-beridden popular novelette written in 1880, tells of a young girl in Lancashire, Hepzibah Crabtree, who encounters in this slender volume no fewer than two deaths and a third person near death. This was undoubtedly the point of the book, and it was sold as such. Melancholy was a fashionable ailment. Pusey, the great

55. *Opposite:* castle tunnel built in a churchyard in Otley, Yorkshire, 'In the memory of the eighteen unfortunate men who lost their lives while engaged in the Construction of the Bramhope Railway Tunnel of the Leeds and Thirsk Railway from 1845 to 1849.' Eighteen men had perished, and this memorial was put up at the expense of James Bray, the contractor, the subcontractors, the agents and the 'workmen employed thereon'.

Oxford churchman, seriously considered never smiling again— except in special cases with children. Wallpapers were designed with such inscriptions as 'Man is born unto travail as the sparks fly upward', painted in black letters on grey. This was suggested for the drawing room! Poetry flourished, such as this extract from James John Hissey's *An old-fashioned journey through England and Wales* (1884):

> Lay me in a Gothic Tomb,
> In whose solemn fretted gloom
> I may lie in wondering state
> With all the grandeur of the great.
> Over me, magnificent,
> Carve a stately monument.
> Then thereon my statue lay,
> With hands in attitude to pray,
> And Angels serve to hold my head,
> Weeping o'er the marble dead.

The age drew to a close with Queen Victoria's white funeral in 1901. She had always wanted this since Tennyson had suggested it to her twenty-eight years before, and she had also decreed that no undertakers were to be present. Her body, in a long white robe

56. *Above:* detail of the canopied tomb, in Kensal Green Cemetery, London W.10., of William Mulready, Royal Academician and Knight of the Legion of Honour, who died in 1863. On the plinth there is a stone-carved frieze showing scenes and implements associated with the life of an artist. (See also Pls. XXI, XXII, 52.)

57. *Above:* the gravestone, in Great Yarmouth, Norfolk, of George Beloe, who was drowned in 1845 when the suspension bridge gave way under the weight of the hundreds of people watching Nelson, the clown being pulled down the river in a wash-tub by three geese. He was advertising Cook's circus and the catastrophe ruined them.

swathed in her wedding veil and strewn with snowdrops, was laid in state for ten days at Osborne before being taken to Windsor. People knelt in the fields as the train went past on that last sad journey from the Isle of Wight, and in London they thronged the purple-and-white-hung streets as the procession, to the strains of Highland laments, Chopin, and Beethoven, bore the Queen's body to Paddington. Perhaps if this curious celebration of death had happened forty or so years earlier, the history of Victorian mourning would have been a totally different one. Certainly, with the Queen's passing, a new age dawned. She joined her beloved Albert four days later at Frogmore.

> Dust to Dust and Ashes to Ashes
> Into the tomb the great Queen dashes

wrote an Indian babu at the time.

Public Houses, Restaurants and Hotels

At an annual general meeting in 1870 of the United Kingdom Alliance, one of the many temperance societies that was flourishing at the time, a Member of Parliament, Sir William Lawson, suggested that rather than send its idle workers to the Colonies, England would do better instead to deport its 150,000 publicans. These were the evil men, he said, who were responsible for the unbridled vice and misery of the working classes.

But in spite of the efforts of Sir William and other such noble-minded citizens, little could be done to stem the flow of liquor. George Cruikshank, the cartoonist, spent many years of his life drawing fearsome warnings. He was himself a teetotaller, attached to the 'Havelock Volunteer Temperance Corps of the Middlesex Rifles Militia', and strove to influence with his wit the 'Devotees' of gin, whose progress 'is marked with desolation, misery and crime'. His cartoons, such as 'The Gin Juggarnath', 'The Worship of Bacchus' and, grimmest of all, a series in two parts entitled 'The Bottle' and 'The Drunkard's Children', were all stern moralistic tracts, priced low to reach those who needed them most. Within days over 100,000 copies of 'The Bottle' had been sold. This series showed how from 'Just . . . a drop' partaken of in the cosy family parlour, total ruin could follow. The same room is shown in deteriorating circumstances and, with all the money having been spent on drink, the youngest child dying of starvation. The husband finally kills his wife with the 'instrument of all their misery'—'The Bottle'. The two elder children are thrown on to the streets, while the father, a maniac, sits trembling in a cage. Both children die in the end, the boy in a threepenny lodging-house, the girl gracefully flying through the air as she throws herself off an ornate bridge.

Most of these moralistic lectures were not seriously heeded. The people delighted in the pursuit of pleasure, and more and more palaces were built for them to enjoy it in. Gin palaces, as they were called—incorrectly as their interests were not only with gin but with spirits generally—dazzled their clients with their inviting opulence. They had to, for not only were there rivals in their own field, but also an ever-increasing abundance of beer- and alehouses trying to outshine and eclipse them. In 1830, the beer duty imposed

107

58, 59. The Vines, Lime Street, Liverpool. Known locally as 'the Big House', this beautiful example of late Victorian elegance was built in 1898–1900 by Walter Thomas (see also Pl. XXXII). *Above:* the saloon bar, showing the enormous oil paintings on the wall and the massive chandeliers. *Left:* detail of one of the great mahogany pillars supporting the ceiling of the private bar.

on the English in the reign of Charles II was abolished. This, together with the new freedom that enabled any taxpayer to sell beer from his premises without a special licence from the magistrates, opened the sluice gates for this 'beverage of purity and quality' to flow through the land. Public feeling had been agitating for some time for legislation to facilitate the sale of beer, since it was far less harmful than spirits but cost very much more. According to John Weale, in *London Exhibited* (1851), beer was considered to be 'a wholesome liquor, which enables London porter drinkers to undergo tasks that a gin drinker would sink under. Happy, indeed, would it have been had they been able, in the early part of this century, when food was dear, and the means of obtaining the necessaries of life almost beyond their reach, if they could have resisted the temptation which was most artfully placed before them, to displace this truly English and wholesome beverage for that ardent spirit gin.' The country was rewarded by the new beer laws. By 1851 the duties on malt and hops produced nearly £5,000,000 annually for the revenue. Ales, sparkling and light, became more popular than the murky porter and its superior version, stout, and pewter mugs were replaced by glass tankards as it became fashionable to drink with the eye as well as with the mouth.

It was a new world of pleasure for many, with more money available to be spent on it. Almost everyone could afford relaxation of some kind. The working man was delighted to be able to escape into the all-male society of the beerhouse, with its sawdust and spitoons, for a convivial puff at a hired-out clay pipe, spending a penny on the brass tobacco box—'one penny, one twist'. These were the only places where you could escape from the lavish decoration, too, for, apart from the modest interiors of these humble beerhouses, the embellishment of public places of pleasure had gone wild. Restaurants, hotels, cafés and, most elaborate of all, public houses glittered from floor to ceiling with cut glass, beaten brass, mosaics, mahogany and leather. The designers' fancies knew no bounds, vulgarity was positively encouraged and ostentation flourished.

Liverpool, which has retained many of her nineteenth-century pub interiors, can boast of having two of the most splendid in the whole of England—the Philharmonic and the Vines (known locally as the Big House). The Philharmonic was built between 1898 and 1900 by Walter Thomas. It has a semi-circular mahogany bar inlaid with a panel of red, gold, orange, blue and green mosaic which sweeps round its full length. The floor is mosaic, and round the mahogany walls there are bands of beaten copper, showing willowy medieval figures playing various musical instruments. There is a mass of both stained and cut glass and the ceiling drips with pendants. In addition to this bar, there are three more rooms, each with their own individual character: one small and panelled, another with a large stained-glass window taking up the whole of one wall. Beyond these is the overwhelmingly beautiful saloon bar. This is an enormous room, with chandeliers, 6-foot-high golden artichokes decorating the top of the walls, beaten brass panels of animals at eye level, mahogany panelled walls and sculptured naked women supporting the ceiling—in all, a glistening and gleaming fairyland. The Vines is a marginally more sedate establishment, with splendid oil paintings which give it a dignity more associated with a private house.

The sophistication of a capital city has kept many in London intact: the Princess Louise in High Holborn, with rows of flower-patterned mirrors in the bar upstairs, and an elegant grey marble gentlemen's lavatory downstairs; the Swan in Hammersmith, with the mosaic swan enclosed in a dutch gable, its white feathers glistening in the sun against the gold background; the King's Head at Tooting, with its mass of glittering cut glass and mahogany; and the Beehive at Brentford, with its gleaming ceramic exterior. In the Tottenham, Oxford Street, London, there are tiled friezes, ceiling paintings framed in plaster, exquisitely and brightly painted mirrors framed in mahogany and, most unusually, fake tapestries, where oil paints have been applied to tapestry weave. In

60. *Below:* the Swan, King Street, London W.6. This massive red-brick building dates from 1901. At the corner it is surmounted by mosaic Dutch gables.

Right: the Princess Louise, 208–209 gh Holborn, London W.C.1. The pub st received its licence in 1875 and was modelled in 1891. The architect was thur Chitty. It has a lavish interior th, downstairs, the gentlemen's vatory and its marvellous washbasin hich is shown here), urinal stalls and ed floor and walls matching the lendour of the bars. Upstairs there are ws of painted mirrors, by Richard orris & Son of Kennington Road, rrounded by decorative tiles by W. B. mpson.

Below: the Beehive, 227 High Street, entford, Middlesex. Rebuilt in the rly 1900s with an extravagant blue ed Doulton exterior, it stands on the e of the 1848 Britannia.

Manchester, too, at the Crown and Kettle, 6-foot-deep Gothic pendants still hang from an extraordinarily ornate Gothic ceiling. But sometimes this recognition of nineteenth-century splendour has come too late, producing distressing examples of modernized pubs which have been re-Victorianized.

Our old friend John Claudius Loudon, in his *Encyclopedia of Cottage, Farm and Villa Architecture and Furniture*, declared that the country inn was also an architectural issue of great importance: 'Our opinion is, that, with the advancement of civilization, country inns . . . will, as architectural objects, rank next to buildings for public offices.' He saw grandiose possibilities: 'Inns of Recreation seem destined to contain all the comforts and luxuries which are now almost exclusively to be found in the mansions and palaces of the aristocracy of Europe; . . . Such inns will, therefore, not be confined to indoor conveniences, but will embrace also all that can be afforded by gardens, pleasure grounds, parks, forests and farms; all the sports of the field, and all the games and exercises that have been known to contribute to human gratification.'

He insisted that in all the inns built, 'whether large or small, there ought to be a library of books . . . among the conveniences, there should be hot, cold, saline, vapour, and hot-air baths.' He suggested that they should be built in all manner of elaborate styles, including the 'Italian' and the 'Swiss'. The 'Italian' had an immense open-arched campanile, reached by a great covered walk sweeping up around the tower. This design is described as 'very picturesque and well calculated for a public house of recreation in a country commanding fine views.' The Swiss chalet is small and covered from top to toe with a multitude of balustrades, balls and spikes of wood. 'A tea garden', at 'a small country inn', he writes of as 'pleasing', where 'alcoves may be formed of trellis-work, and covered with honeysuckle, virgin's bower and other creeping shrubs.' He recommends that all inns have a bowling green, by which an elegant banqueting hall may be erected!

The *Encyclopedia* also considers detailed plans of working interiors and shows designs of furniture in the most ornate cast-iron Gothic. On the subject of inn signs, he proposes 'as substitutes for the common daubs now generally stuck up, excellent oil paintings by superior artists, protected from the weather by projecting cornices; handsome statues of public characters placed on pedestals, or over the entrance porch or portico; or medallions of celebrated men affixed to obelisks.'

When Loudon talks of 'inns' he is using the old-fashioned name for hotels, although the bar was certainly an important feature in these as well. By the 1830s, 'inns' had become 'hotels', 'taverns' were 'restaurants', and 'gin palaces' and 'beer- and alehouses' were 'pubs'. There were new influences from abroad, either brought by *émigrés* or promoted by their sophisticated imi-

3. The Crown and Kettle, Oldham Road, Manchester. Outside, the building is constructed in the nineteenth-century dour late Gothic style in stone, while inside there is an ornate Gothic ceiling with fan vaulting. The great falling pendants were for gasoliers.

tators; as well as 'restaurants' and 'hotels', the new French words 'café' and 'buffet' had crept in.

The advent of the railway also affected the business of public entertaining. As the public house became a less and less respectable place to stay in, there was a growing demand for hotels to be built in all cities to accommodate the ever-increasing number of travellers. By the 1860s, every commercial centre could boast of its 'Station Hotel', its 'Imperial' or its 'Grand'. But it was not just commerce that encouraged the spread of such opulence: the desire for enjoyment, and the money that could be made from supplying it, played just as big a part. One of the great pleasures discovered at this time was the seaside. It was a new experience for thousands, and seaside resorts were actually created by the railway lines leading to them. They sprang up all over the place and, with them, some of the biggest hotel-building projects in the country. In 1862, the Cliff Hotel Company was formed to build 'The Grand' in Scarborough. It was not finished until 1867: the financial outlay was so enormous that the first development company collapsed in 1865, when only the shell of the building was standing. The design was by Cuthbert Broderick, who (*The Building News* reported) 'treats us to the palace of Aladdin of our youth, only considerably increased since then. That, if we recollect all right, had only one dome; now we have four roc's eggs and more; each capped by its own particular incubator . . .' Inside all was decorated in white and gold with amber silk upholstery, and in the two drawing rooms (one of which was 110 × 80 feet) there were four giant bronze statues, each holding twenty lamps. It was a splendid palace, but apparently not particularly exceptional, as the same report goes on to say: 'The rest of the building is of ordinary hotel character but counterchanged; heretofore they have generally been red with white facings. This puts on a sort of bandsman's uniform of white faced with red.' But there was never a hotel exterior architecturally like any other. Each vied with its neighbour for ever greater splendour, in an ostentatious display of architectural luxury—for example, the Russell and the Imperial Hotels in Russell Square, London, two ornate palaces a stone's throw away from each other.

The biggest hotel in the world in its time was the Cecil in London; it opened in 1896 and it outsplendoured them all: Doulton tiles in friezes decorated the superb marble staircase which, with marble banisters, marble rails and marble steps, swept up through great marble-pillared marble arches; the walls were also of marble up to the level of the picture rails. Palms in huge jardinières were everywhere, immense mahogany-pillared and corniced doors

64-6. The Russell Hotel, Russell Square, London W.C.1. Designed in 1898–1900 by Charles Fitzroy Doll, this hotel was opened on Derby Day. These details show its sumptuous interior. *Below left:* the richly decorated ceiling of the Wharncliffe suite, supported by life-size caryatids on plinths (see also Pl. 67). *Below right:* the pink and brown marble pillars and sculptured plaster panels in the hall. *Opposite:* the arches leading off to the hall.

glittered with their panels of mirrors and *trompe l'oeil* wallpaper. The design of this paper was on an enormous scale, in the Classical style, and appeared wherever possible between the rich embellishments. The dining rooms, reception rooms and the billiard and smoking rooms were equally splendid; they all had Doulton tile decorations, and the smoking rooms were designed in the Indian style. The whole building was demolished in 1930.

The St. Pancras Hotel is one of the few great piles that have remained intact, probably more by luck than by good management. The graceful interweaving cast-iron staircases are still there, but are used only as a means of getting to and from British Rail offices. The original wallpaper still glows scarlet and gold, soaring up to the great frescoed stone ceiling vaults, and the original carpet is still underfoot. Even the radiator covers, made of charmingly patterned cast iron, merit a visit. The hotel was built between 1868 and 1875 and was designed by Sir George Gilbert Scott, perhaps somewhat incommodiously since he allowed only four bathrooms to six hundred bedrooms! But many of the large rooms had splendid stone fireplaces, and no doubt the hot coals brought to each guest by the bucketful every morning, along with the bronze pitchers of hot water, as they lay in their brass beds under their linen bedspreads in their anaglypta embossed rooms, partly com-

Overleaf: the splendid Grecian
nple, one of the Abercorn
oms of the Great Eastern Hotel,
ndon E.C.2., which were added
Barry's 1884 building by
lonel R. W. Edis in 1901.
though once threatened with
molition, these rooms are now
ing to be retained, and British
il plan to spend £100,000 on the
tel over the next ten years. (See
so Pls. XXXIII–XXXV.)

pensated for the discomforts caused by the lack of a bath. At least each room contained a chamber pot on a marble stand in the corner.

There were railway hotels in every city by the end of the nineteenth century—splendid affluent gateways through which to pass. The great charm of Victorian hotels, however, was that, although grand, they managed to create a sympathetic and homely atmosphere. As Loudon said, 'a traveller who stays in them, with plenty of money, may enjoy many of the comforts of home, without its cares.' The drawing room of the Great Western Hotel at Paddington was a perfect example of the spirit that was striven for. Dignified yet cosy, it had great palms in corner china pots, a piano with a chintz-covered stool, chintz-skirted armchairs, little round bamboo tables with books on them, standard lamps, a chandelier, vases of flowers and a marble mantel clock. By contrast, the elegant dining room was extremely formal. Splendid pillared framed mirrors reflected the two levels of windows which were interspaced with allegorical figures, and an enormous chandelier hung from the centre of the ceiling, each of the many bulbs shaded with a pretty glass frill. This hotel was damaged during the Second World War and has been largely modernized.

The Great Eastern Hotel, at Liverpool Street Station, is all splendour. When the hotel, which was designed by Barry in 1884, was remodelled in 1901, the *Morning Advertiser* described it as 'unquestionably the most palatial in London'. There are nine exceptionally fine rooms. The Hamilton hall, 100 × 42 feet, and 23 feet high, is a banqueting chamber, thickly plastered and based on the model of the Hôtel Soubise in Paris. This plaster was originally covered with gold leaf. The Abercorn bar, said by a contemporary to 'possess a brilliancy rarely found east of Charing Cross', has a magnificent ceiling of painted plaster in imitation of Spanish leather, while the Norfolk room, with delightful painted panels, possessed in its heyday, according to a contemporary brochure, a 'canopied grill, itself unique of its kind, with pilasters in Brèche violet marble'. The dining room has an immense stained-glass dome; originally the ceiling around this was supported by red scagliola columns but these are now painted over. The Middlesex room has great pedimented doors; the Essex room has a wooden overmantel, built around the clock, reaching to the ceiling; the Beaufort room is delicately plastered; and, finally, there are two of the most curious rooms in London—the Grecian and Egyptian temples. They were built as masonic temples and are quite remarkable. The Grecian is a mass of sumptuous marble pillars, floors, walls and pediments, and you descend a curved marble staircase into it. The Egyptian is unique in its subtlety: murals in muted colours depict strange and magical scenes, there are tapered Egyptian doors and an immense gold-painted organ.

Opposite: detail of one of the
luptuous caryatids which
pport the moulded beams of the
nelled ceiling of the Wharncliffe
ite in the Russell Hotel (see
. 64).

By the middle of the century, it had become respectable to eat out and restaurants responded to their new clientele by decorating themselves in a suitable fashion. At Frascati's in Oxford Street, London, there was a private dining room with magnificent ceramic murals on every wall. These tiles were designed by W. J. Neatby of Doultons at Lambeth, and they were all painted in bright colours, giving the room an 'especially festive air', according to a contemporary report.

Frascati's was only one among hundreds of such restaurants throughout the country, but only very few now remain intact. A coffee room in Leeds had a vast ceramic mural of a beautifully-robed Turkish lady, life-size, lying on a pile of cushions. In Houghton-le-Spring, County Durham, an ice-cream parlour had cut glass and mahogany box pews on either side of long narrow marble tables on curved cast-iron legs. It was all replaced in the 1960s by speckled pale green and grey formica throughout. The case of the Café Royal in Edinburgh, however, is an example of how positive action can prevent such destruction. Its beautiful stained-glass windows showing life-size Victorian sportsmen (the delicacy of the angler's hands alone is worth the journey) in the buffet bar, and the Doulton-tiled murals of scientists and discoverers in the public bar were under threat of demolition in 1969.

69. *Above:* the Plymouth Grove Hotel, Plymouth Grove, Chorlton-on-Medlock, Manchester. Dating from the late nineteenth century, this brick building has an enormous free-standing clock tower; the clock face is pedimented and surmounted by an open lantern.

70. *Opposite:* Doulton tile picture of the first Cunarder, Umbria, and a Liverpool paddle-steamer, in the Café Royal, Register Place, Edinburgh (see also Pl. XXVI). This has a perfect, unspoilt Victorian interior, dating from 1862, by Robert Paterson. The great public bar is surrounded by Doulton tile pictures of Victorian inventors, and cast-iron pillars support the ceiling.

71, 72. *Opposite:* the Elephant public house, St. Nicholas Street, Bristol. This was built in 1867 on the site of the original Elephant, which dated from the sixteenth century. The trunk of the original hanging sign was sawn off when the first building came down and built into the wall above the entrance of the Victorian pub. *Above:* the Elephant and Castle, 2 South Lambeth Place, Vauxhall, London S.W.8. Dating from the 1870s, the architect of this curious mixture of classical motifs is unknown.

73. *Right:* the Midland Hotel, Peter Street, Manchester. This was designed in 1898 by Charles Trubshaw. A massive building of granite and terracotta, this detail shows how the rainwater pipes were made an integrated part of the façade.

Woolworths needed the site to enlarge their nearby store. 8,700 people signed a petition in protest and after two years of battling and a lot of publicity it was finally decided not to demolish the building.

Apart from the fanaticism of preservationists, there is a growing awareness within the trade that the Victorian pubs, hotels and restaurants were built with sound commercial acumen, their decorative extravagance and style being an essential part of the luxury of being publicly entertained. The Randolph Hotel in Oxford, designed by William Wilkinson in 1864, was elaborately re-Victorianized in 1974. A full circle has been turned—but at a sad cost.

74. Five sculpted Prime Ministers' heads decorate the façade of the Openshaw Inn, Ashton Old Road, Manchester. The Brewers' Association had scheduled this pub, which stands in the middle of an industrial development, for demolition but, after reassessment, it is now to be retained.

Shops

It can safely be said that in five years' time there will be a mere handful of small Victorian shops left in England. In the name of progress, these buildings of undeniable charm and curiosity are being demolished as fast as it is possible for their owners to get at them. Uniform dullness on a massive scale, of chromium, plastic, linoleum and vinyl, is taking the place of the unfailingly original, colourful and curious interiors of the last century, whose gleaming surfaces of mahogany, brass, glass and marble made veritable little palaces out of every shop.

Old stalwarts like Lipton's, Home and Colonial and the Maypole Dairies, who seemed, comfortingly, to be persevering with their distinguished elegance, are soon to go as well. With a policy of modernizing every original branch in the next few years, Allied Suppliers, now controlled by Cavenham (under whom these three now operate), are hard at it, with the rich tiled and mahogany interiors currently being replaced by a uniform formica surface. Their original names are to disappear as well: 'Lipton', with its stark, modernized leaf design, is to incorporate all three. This is surely a sad and shortsighted policy; no one could deny the splendour of the firms' names in their original richly-cut golden letters, and the argument that hailed the tile as the most suitable and decorative surface still stands. Why then replace them, tile for tile, with characterless modern alternatives? The men who created these vast empires would be outraged by this travesty of their original conceptions.

Sir Thomas Lipton, most flamboyant of them all, had a series of specially-designed tiles made for his establishments: shamrocks intertwining with £s (Ls for Lipton's; £s for sterling) in combinations of rich greens and creams. In a Lipton's branch at Berwick-on-Tweed, now demolished, dark green marble counters were supported by lustrous sweeps of dark green shamrocks, the dado behind was of green and cream, and the walls rose up in the same pattern, but only in cream. Lipton's Glasgow 'market' (so-called to emphasize its contact with the working man) had a vast horseshoe-shaped mahogany counter, about 100 feet long, and the Paisley branch, again with a 'horseshoe' counter, was illuminated by sixty gas jets.

Sir Thomas was the first entrepreneur to introduce tea into the country as an everyday commmodity rather than as a luxury item. With his slogan 'Direct from tea-garden to tea pot', he sold tea from his own plantations in Ceylon for one shilling a pound that was of the same quality as that which could fetch thirty-six guineas a pound at the Mincing Lane London tea auctions! To advertise the first shipment's arrival in 1889, Sir Thomas (then Mr. Lipton—he was knighted by Queen Victoria in 1896) arranged for 200 men, bearing 80 tons of tea, to parade through Glasgow's streets in authentic Singhalese costume. His advertising was always extravagantly elaborate. 'Lipton's Orphans'—pigs bought for the business and proclaimed by men with great banners—were paraded through the streets with 'Lipton' painted on their backs. In 1881 a giant cheese, weighing three tons, was drawn round Glasgow by an elephant. Seven years later Lipton offered a five-ton cheese to the Queen for the Jubilee celebrations, but she refused to accept it. 'Sky Telegrams'—'pound' notes emblazoned with Lipton's portrait and the promise to give the bearer goods to the value of one pound for fifteen shillings—were scattered from balloons, tableaux were sculptured in butter, and thin men were made to carry banners 'Going to Liptons', while fat men carried banners 'Coming from Liptons'—this last stunt developed into concave and

76, 77. *Opposite, left:* the meat hall of Harrods, Knightsbridge, London, 1901 (see also Pl. XXXVII The counters were made of pink, brown, black, cream and white marble imported from Sicily. *Opposite, right:* a detail of one of the tiled tableaux in A. G. Hedges, Butcher, Chiswick High Road, London W.4. By J. S. Boutal of Hammersmith, they depict farm scenes in blue and white with brown 'marble' borders.

5. *Opposite:* the 'L' of Sir Thomas Lipton's ceramic tiles on one of his shops in Berwick-upon-Tweed. In cream or green, they have decorated his shops all over the country since 1871. This shop was pulled down in the 1960s.

convex mirrors being hung outside the shops, the first making you miserably thin, the second excessively fat!

The time was ripe for such extravagance in retail trading. A spirit of development, of change and expansion was in the air. Industrial wealth, creating a new spending population—the middle classes ever out to maintain their improved situation, and the poorer classes now receiving regular wage packets—presented the ambitious individual with a field ripe for opportunity. Sir Thomas Lipton, David Greig, Henry C. Harrod, Peter Robinson, William Whiteley, Arthur Lasenby Liberty, John James Sainsbury, Michael Marks and Tom Spencer, Peter Jones, Emerson Muschamp Bainbridge and Mr. J. J. Fenwick of Newcastle, Isaac Merrit Singer of Glasgow, Thomas Kendal and James Milne of Manchester and Thomas Burberry of Basingstoke—they all had their beginnings in this prosperous latter half of the nineteenth century. The population had multiplied on an unprecedented scale, doubling, in the second half of the century, from 20 to 40 million. A vast, new affluent society had to be catered for. Ready with their money, and wanting something to show for it, they were eager to harvest the rich crops sewn by Mr. William Whiteley, 'the Universal Provider', Sir Thomas and the like. Whiteleys, selling anything from 'a pin to an elephant', was opened as a small haber-

dashers in Westbourne Grove in 1863, with, as the years went by, further shops being added to house new departments—one, for goods from the Orient, followed in the footsteps of Arthur Liberty.

The majority of the great purchasing palaces started in the same way, as small haberdashers or drapers. Peter Robinson came south from Yorkshire and in 1833 opened a linen drapers shop in Oxford Street, while Mr. Swan and Mr. Edgar had even humbler beginnings: they met as drapery stall holders. But the pioneer, the founder of the true department store (rather than the vast clothing emporium, such as Peter Robinson's) was Emerson Muschamp Bainbridge of Newcastle-upon-Tyne. Starting out as a drapers in 1838, Bainbridge's was also, according to Alison Adburghham in *Shops and Shopping* (1964), probably the first establishment to sell ready-made dresses for women. 'Sewed muslin dresses' were advertised to a public which had until then had to buy by the yard, sewing every stitch themselves.

Harrods was one of the few exceptions to these humble beginnings, although its origins were almost as modest: it was a grocer's shop that Henry Charles Harrod bought in the village of Knightsbridge in 1849. Expanding it to the point that 'Everything, London' was a justifiable telegraphic address and having the first moving staircase in England, Harrods was brought to its well-known splendour of today. Of all these great stores Harrods was the most lavishly decorated. The meat hall, with tiles by W. J. Neatby, is a great glimmering cavern of marble and ceramics, which still maintains today, as it must have done in 1901, the highest standards, with superb arrangements of fish, meat, fowl and game for sale. The counters are of pink and white marble, the floors of black and white, and high above in the great roof is the staggering display of Art Nouveau tiles by Neatby. Great richly coloured, stylized trees are split open down their trunks to reveal hunting and farmyard scenes, with peacocks standing on either side of each one, the trunks arising out of brightly coloured, swirling, fish-filled waters.

As the prosperity grew, both large and small shops began to embellish their establishments, much to the consternation of Dickens who, in *Sketches by Boz* (1836), protested in flowing terms that:

It is a very remarkable circumstance, that different trades appear to partake of the disease to which elephants and dogs are especially liable, and to run stark, staring mad periodically. The great distinction between the animals and the trades, is, that the former run mad with a certain degree of propriety—they are very regular in their irregularities . . . if an elephant runs mad, we are all ready for him—kill or cure—pills or bullets—calomel in conserve of roses, or lead in a musket barrel. If a dog happens to look unpleasantly warm in the summer months, and to trot about the shady side of the street with a quarter of a yard of tongue hanging out of his mouth, a thick leather muzzle . . . is instantly clapped over his head . . . and he either looks remarkably unhappy for the next six weeks, or becomes legally insane, and goes as it were, by Act of Parliament. But these trades are as eccentric as comets; nay, worse, for no one can calculate on the recurrence of the strange appearances which betoken the disease . . . Six or eight years ago, the epidemic began to display itself among the linen drapers and haberdashers. The primary symptoms were an inordinate love of plate glass, and a passion for gas lights and gilding. The disease gradually progressed, and at last attained a fearful height. Quiet, dusty, old shops in different parts of the town were pulled down; spacious premises with stuccoed fronts and gold letters were erected instead; floors were covered with Turkey carpets; roofs supported by massive pillars; doors knocked into windows, a dozen squares of glass into one, one shopman into a dozen . . . Suddenly it burst out again among the chemists; the symptoms were the same, with the addition of a strong desire to stick the Royal Arms over the shop door, and a great race for mahogany, varnish, and

. All that remained of a fish shop,
is block of tiles was attached to
e end of a terrace of houses in
tton-le-Hole, County Durham.

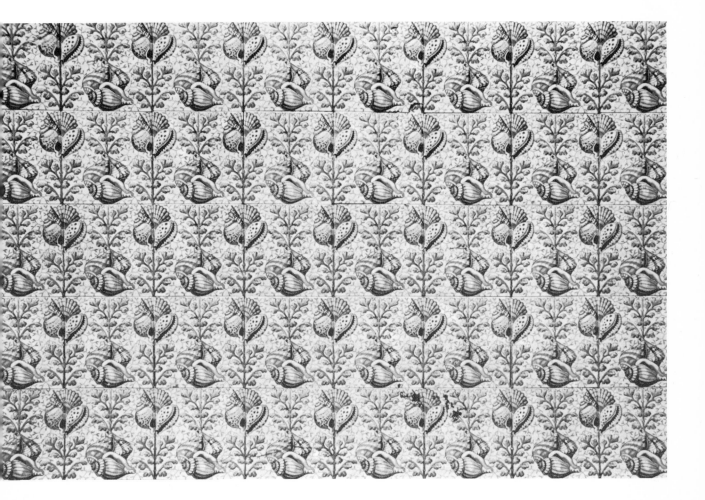

81. *Opposite:* interior of Sainsburys, High Street, Oxford. This was in fact built in 1910 but the original patterns the Minton tiles that were designed fo Sainsburys in 1882 were used, and the mosaic floor was laid by Italian craftsmen. The shop was bought by Lloyd's Bank in 1973 and the façade is be retained, but there is doubt about t fate of the interior, which now stands empty.

79. *Left:* Blue and white twisted pillars with composite capitals decorate the façade of a United Dairies shop in the High Street, Wimbledon, London S.W.19. This dates from the early 1900s and was originally Southdown Dairies.

80. *Below:* Tiled tableau of Britannia on the façade of Longbone and Sons, 112 Marygate, Berwick-upon-Tweed. Originally built in the early 1900s as a fish shop, it was completely tiled inside and out by Duncans of Glasgow. The whole of the tiled interior is now hidden. Carpets cover the floors, walls and ceilings and the shop now sells tartans.

expensive floor-cloths. Then the hosiers were infected, and began to pull down their shop-fronts with frantic recklessness.

Nevertheless, despite Dickens' attack, shops throughout the land continued to be decorated in their hundreds.

A grocer's shop in Newcastle-upon-Tyne had a number of mahogany barley-sugar-stick poles rising out of a rich semi-circular mahogany counter to meet an ornate shelf above. The goods were stored behind the counter in polished wooden compartments, great hams and cheeses hung in the windows, and coffee beans and crystallized pineapples were sold loose by the door. An immense yellow barrel of butter stood on the counter. This shop survived until it was demolished for road widening in the late 1960s. Ten miles away, in Hetton-le-Hole, a whole tiled tableau from a fish-shop wall stood for years against the end of a terrace of houses; the shop had gone but the great blue and white wall of seaweed and shells remained. In a sweet shop in Barnes, London, a delightful oak cash desk is still intact, with stained-glass windows of birds, fruit and blossoms let into panels; around the corner, in Church Road, an excellent conversion has taken place, giving us a faint ray of hope for the future. Half a butcher's shop, with an enchantingly pretty tiled interior, has been taken over by a busi-

82. Tiled tableau by Carter & Co. of Poole, Dorset, in F. Harvey Ltd., Fishmongers, 46 Norwich Road, Ipswich. Now used as a storeroom, this 1897 tableau has been retained.

ness selling sheets and towels. All the flowered tableaux have been left, sympathetically surrounded by Edwardian patterned anaglypta paper which covers the undoubtedly unsuitable (in its new role) expanses of plain white ceramic. These can still be seen next door, with the sawdusted wooden floor and magnificent great butcher's blocks. The exterior is superb, with extravagantly curling, rich golden letters.

Tiles played a major part in the decoration of nineteenth-century shops. Basically, there were three different types of tiles for this commercial use: those that were hand-painted, those that were transfer-printed, and those that were in majolica. Butchers, fishmongers and dairies led the way predominantly; specially-commissioned hand-painted tiles were decorated for the proprietor by artists in 'art pottery studios'. If you wanted a larger area covered, with a correspondingly large pattern, transfer-printing produced the best results, as the impression was more even than that produced by hand-painting; but for rich lustrous luxury, majolica led the field, its sculptured shapes rising over the surfaces. Sainsbury's and David Greig's had superb ceramic interiors, Sainsbury's with massive marble counters supported by glowing brown tiles of different hues in majolica and plain glaze. The rich ceramic walls, dadoes and friezes, in dark, bright and olive green, cream, white and brown, rose from the mosaic floor right up to the ceiling, presenting a superb, sumptuous and perfectly finished whole. In Ipswich, there is an immense tiled scene, some 15 feet long. It shows men in plus fours and gaiters out shooting with their dogs. A pile of dead pheasants lies beside them, while another is being shot down from the sky.

As well as tiling, other plans were afoot for the decoration of these new symbols of prosperity. In an architectural book of engravings of suggested shop fronts, *Street Architecture* (1885), the authors, Victor Delasseux and John Elliott, realizing that 'a marked improvement is taking place generally in the decorative arts, in which Architecture, in its application to trading purposes, participates', wrote that they hoped by this volume to encourage and excite their 'more eminent professional brethren' to contribute 'by bringing out works of their own on this really important branch of Art . . . It may not at first sight appear a very dignified employment for the heads of the profession, to use their talents in designing shop fronts and street façades, but in reality, few classes of subjects afford such scope for inventive genius, and none where its efforts would be more appreciated, or exercise so favourable an influence on the taste of the multitude.'

Then follows a series of ornate and minutely detailed plates of shop fronts in the Classical, Renaissance and Gothic styles. The 'Hall' for the tea dealer and grocer, where 'the timber employed should be oak or its imitation', the hatter, general outfitter and

hosier, and the boot and shoe manufacturer are all in elaborate domestic Gothic. The boot- and shoemaker's shop shows a grim collection of heads—lions, kings, gargoyles and ladies—carved beneath an imposing high balcony supported by consoles. The grocer was advised that it 'will add much to the effect, if the mouldings and the foliations, and the bands of the carved arrises be gilt'. For the shoemaker: 'The taste of the gentlemen following this profession is so decidedly Classical, as evidenced by the Greek names given to all their inventions in leather, that it ought perhaps to have induced us to design à la Grecque, but the recollection that wooden shoes preceded calf, decided the question in favour of timber.' The ironmonger and brazier, the butcher, the bookseller, the poulterer and the chemist, the paper hanger and decorator, and the seedsman—all were given the most detailed consideration. The 'rustic' style was considered the most suitable for such a business as the poulterer, while a Gothic iron fantasy was suggested for the ironmonger and brazier. 'A little extra expense in the façade will not be thrown away in this business, the front affording the best opportunity of shewing what the proprietor can affect with the material in which he deals.'

From the indoor market to the individual shop, from the multiple chain to the department store, all types of shops flourished in

86-8. *Opposite:* J. Musk, Butcher, High Street, Newmarket, Cambridge. This was converted from a china shop in the early 1900s by the present owner's step-grandfather. The original floors, walls and counters remain. *Above:* Carters, 211–217 Old Kent Road, London S.E.1., gentlemen's outfitter since 1851, when Mr. Carter displayed his hats in a showcase on stilts in the front garden of No. 215. The whole block was developed in the 1860s to form the entire store, which is Classical in style, with a stone balustrade decorated with stone pineapples and lions. The clock *(left)*, which used to be mechanical, is now electric and the bowler rises the relevant number of times on the hour. The mural of babies sailing the seas in Carters' hats *(right)* used to be their trademark. This block, together with the surrounding sites, has recently been bought from the Rolls Estate by the London Borough of Southwark, who intend to demolish the existing building.

this age of retailing adventure. No wonder the Victorians saw fit to celebrate it with such loving care.

Sadly, there are very few of these shops left. Those that do still exist are mainly small family firms, establishments where 'a kind and obliging manner' still prevails, a manner that 'carried with it an indescribable charm' (advice given to shopkeepers, in *Enquire within upon Everything*, 1869). James Smith, umbrella manufacturers of New Oxford Street, London; J. Musk, butcher of High Street, Newmarket; D. Hall, general drapers of Stroud Green, London; T. Hayward, china and glass dealer of Deansgate, Manchester; and Carters, outfitters of the Old Kent Road, London—all survive. These are family firms in the best tradition, with the original civility as well as the original architecture intact.

Conclusion

I n the light of its quality and variety, Victorian decoration can have few critics amongst its enemies, and to its friends it is pure joy. We still live our daily lives surrounded by so much of it, despite the appalling extent of the destruction of nineteenth-century buildings. Indeed it is because of the very familiarity of their comforting backdrop that we do tend to take them for granted. The aim of this book is to open more people's eyes to these glories that are everywhere, and make them want to save whatever they can from being destroyed when some inadequate modern substitute is planned. Modern substitutes can so often be inadequate. In Sheffield, for example, a skyscraper hotel has vile orange formica panels, dirty and split, buckling away from the passage walls. Shopping precincts everywhere have the same soulessness and smell. The quality of workmanship is cheapening on so many levels. Concrete, miserable faceless concrete, is a major aesthetic offender, able to create not only visual tattiness, but also buildings that are quite out of scale with the rest of our towns and cities. A blindingly offensive example of this is the un-relieved solid grey wall of the Stock Exchange that rises up to first-floor level in Throgmorton Street in the City of London. The contrast between nineteenth-century architectural variety and twentieth-century architectural monotony is encapsulated in this one street. On the left (looking north) there is a variety of gables, bay, arched, pedimented and round windows, caryatids supporting the pediments of doors, the mosaic lettering of *Slater's Restaurant*, the gold lettering of *Throgmorton Restaurant*, archways into what were once courtyards (now to be replaced by more tower blocks) and graceful hanging lamps. On the right there is a solid blank block.

All the subjects covered in this book have suffered, and are suffering, from a serious reversal of quality. If only the panic of obligatory modernization could be tempered down. To see what is happening to many hotels, simply go to Russell Square in London, where the Imperial and the Russell Hotels, two Victorian terra-cotta palaces, once stood side by side. The original Imperial was demolished in 1966 and rebuilt, while the Russell has been re-stored. The contrast is astonishing: the Imperial is tawdry, with

138

nasty gold mosaic panels stuck on to already stained concrete blocks, while the Russell is all splendour, with marble walls, marble floors and a marble staircase.

Shops are suffering most of all, with formica and steel taking the place of mahogany and brass, and an asphyxiating smell of plastic replacing a maze of interweaving aromas. There are a few establishments that soldier on, proud of their tradition, but their number is dwindling. The visual disaster of shop fronts and supermarkets is well known. Until very recently, Hungerford in Berkshire had a delightful butcher's shop with a ceramic and pillared exterior in muted reds and greens that blended perfectly with the street. This was torn down and replaced by a new white front with plastic letters and a mass of plate glass; it is now ferociously out of tune with its surroundings and jars horribly with the general mellowness of the town.

The shortcomings of railway stations built today are also particularly visible. They were built in the nineteenth century as focal points of the towns and cities, magnificent symbols of the railway age, and modern counterparts, understandably not built with the same degree of adulation, now sit on these same sites in undeserved prominence. Euston is a perfect example and Oxford is another one: both are mean low buildings, sadly unworthy of their cities.

Street furniture now offends rather than complements every street, with forests of plastic, glass, fibreboard and tin growing down most of them. In contrast with the meticulous care taken in the nineteenth century, there now seems to be little attempt to harmonize street furniture with its surroundings.

Cemeteries and graveyards are grim places today, with their stark lawns and rows of faceless marble blocks, providing neither the landscaped nor the sculptural relief that the Victorians gave them. If only some of these beautiful nineteenth-century tracts of land, which have now fallen into such terrible decay, could be utilized to provide some much needed green relief to our towns and cities. The London Borough of Southwark, however, has recognized this potential and at Nunhead Cemetery it is going to retain 29 of the 50 acres as a nature reserve. Everything will be left as it is, apart from removing any gravestone that might be dangerous, and thinning out undergrowth 'only to the extent desirable to preserve the flora and fauna'. The rest, with landscaped tombstones and trees, will remain.

So there is still hope, but let us try not to take the nineteenth-century architecture around us too much for granted.

Bibliography

Decorative Detail

Barnard, J. *The Decorative Tradition.* Architectural Press, London 1973.

Betjeman, Sir J. *First and Last Loves.* John Murray, London 1952.

—— *Ghastly Good Taste.* Chapman & Hall, London 1933.

Booker, C., and Lycett-Green, C. *Goodbye London.* Collins, London 1973.

Builder, The. London 1846, 1847, 1858, 1864, 1881.

Building News, The. London 1864.

Gloag, J. *Mr. Loudon's England.* Oriel Press, Newcastle-upon-Tyne 1970.

—— *Victorian Taste.* David & Charles, Newton Abbot 1962.

Gomme, A., and Walker, D. *The Architecture of Glasgow.* Lund Humphries, London 1968.

Hissey, J. J. *Across England in a Dog Cart.* Richard Bentley & Son, London 1891.

Hobhouse, H. *Lost London.* Macmillan, London 1971.

Hughes, Q. *Seaport.* Lund Humphries, London 1964.

Jones, B. *Follies and Grottoes.* Constable, London 1953.

Jones, O. *Grammar of Ornament.* Bernard Quaritch, London 1856.

Loudon, J. C. *Encyclopaedia of Cottage, Farm and Villa Architecture and Furniture.* Longman, Rees, Orme, Brown, Green & Longman, London 1833.

Physick, J., and Darby, M. *Marble Halls.* Victoria & Albert Museum, London 1973.

Price, Sir U. *On the Picturesque.* Caldwell, Lloyd & Co., Edinburgh 1842.

Priestly, J. B. *Victoria's Heyday.* Heinemann, London 1972.

Pugin, A. W. *An Apology for the Revival of Christian Architecture in England.* John Weale, London 1843.

Richardson, C. J. *Picturesque Designs for Mansions, Villas and Lodges.* Atchley, London 1870.

Ruskin, J. *The Seven Lamps of Architecture.* George Allen & Unwin, London 1889.

Scott, Sir G. G. *Remarks on Secular and Domestic Architecture.* John Murray, London 1858.

Seddon, J. P. *Progress in Art and Architecture with Precedence for Ornament.* David Bogue, London 1852.

Street Furniture

Bracebridge, D. *The Archaeology of the Industrial Revolution.* Heinemann, London 1973.

Builder, The. London 1851, 1891

Building News, The. London 1893.

Lister, R. *Decorative Wrought Iron Work in Great Britain.* Bell, London 1957.

Physick, J., and Darby, M. *Marble Halls.* Victoria & Albert Museum, London 1973.

Railway Stations

Andrews, C. B. *The Railway Age.* Country Life, London 1937.

Barman, C. *Early British Railways.* Penguin, Harmondsworth 1950.

—— *An Introduction to Railway Architecture,* Art & Technics, London 1950.

Biddle, G. *Victorian Stations.* David & Charles, Newton Abbot 1973.

Briggs, A. *Victorian Cities.* Penguin, Harmondsworth 1963.

Builder, The. London 1846, 1854, 1865, 1876, 1879, 1881.

Building News, The. London 1845, 1846, 1863, 1864, 1869, 1877, 1879.

Evans, J. *The Victorians.* Cambridge University Press, Cambridge 1966.

Hobhouse, H. *Lost London.* Macmillan, London 1971.

Holland, H. *Traveller's Architecture.* George Harrap, London 1971.

Klingender, F. D. *Art and the Industrial Revolution.* Carrington, London 1947.

Lloyd, D., and Insell, D. *Railway Station Architecture.* David & Charles, Newton Abbot 1967.

Loudon, J. C. *Encyclopaedia of Cottage, Farm and Villa Architecture and Furniture.* Longman, Rees, Orme, Brown, Green & Longman, London 1833.

Lowerson, J. *Victorian Sussex.* BBC Publications, London 1972.

Meeks, C. *The Railroad Station.* Yale University Press, Newhaven, Conn., 1956; The Architectural Press, London 1957.

Physick, J., and Darby, M. *Marble Halls*. Victoria & Albert Museum, London 1973.

Price, Sir U. *On the Picturesque*. Caldwell, Lloyd & Co., Edinburgh 1842.

Ruskin, J. *The Seven Lamps of Architecture*. George Allen & Unwin, London 1889.

Simmonds, J. *Saint Pancras Station*. George Allen & Unwin, London 1968.

Somervell, D. C. *The Victorian Age*. The Historical Association, 1937.

Symes, R., and Cole, D. *Railway Architecture of Greater London*. Osprey, Reading 1973.

—— *Railway Architecture of the South East*. Osprey, Reading 1972.

Williams, F. S. *Our Iron Roads*. Bemrose & Sons, London and Irongate, Derby, 1852.

Graves Besant, Sir W. *London in the Nineteenth Century*. Adam and Charles Black, London 1909.

Briggs, A. *Victorian Cities*. Penguin, Harmondsworth 1963.

Builder, The. London 1846.

Building News, The. London 1857, 1864.

Bunning, J. B. *Designs for Tombs and Monuments*. London 1839.

Burgess, F. *English Churchyard Memorials*. Lutterworth, London 1963.

Curl, J. S. *The Victorian Celebration of Death*. David & Charles, Newton Abbot 1972.

Evans, H. and M. *The Victorians*. David & Charles, Newton Abbot 1973.

Evans, J. *The Victorians*. Cambridge University Press, Cambridge 1966.

Gomme, A., and Walker, D. *The Architecture of Glasgow*. Lund Humphries, London 1968.

Hissey, J. J. *An Old Fashioned Journey Through England and Wales*. Richard Bentley & Son, London 1884.

Lindley, K. *Of Graves and Epitaphs*. Hutchinson, London 1965.

Longford, E. *Victoria R.I.* Weidenfeld & Nicholson, London 1964.

Loudon, J. C. *On the Laying-out, Planting and Managing of Cemeteries*. London 1843.

Morley, J. *Death, Heaven and the Victorians*. Studio Vista, London 1971.

Priestly, J. B. *Victoria's Heyday*. Heinemann, London 1972.

Watson, R. A. *Crabtree Fold*. T. Woolmer, London 1888.

Public Houses, Restaurants and Hotels Arts Council of Great Britain. *George Cruikshank*. London 1974.

Barnard, J. *The Decorative Tradition*. Architectural Press, London 1973.

—— *Victorian Ceramic Tiles*. Studio Vista, London 1972.

Batchelor, D. *The English Inn*. Batsford, London 1963.

Builder, The. London 1905.

Building News, The. London 1867.

Burke, J. *The English Inn*. Herbert Jenkins, London 1930.

Hobhouse, H. *Lost London*. Macmillan, London 1971.

Hughes, Q. *Seaport*. Lund Humphries, London 1964.

Loudon, J. C. *Encyclopaedia of Cottage, Farm and Villa Architecture and Furniture*. Longman, Rees, Orme, Brown, Green & Longman, London 1833.

Richardson, A. E. *The Old Inns of England*. Batsford, London 1934.

Richardson, A. E., and Ebeblein, H. D. *The English Inn, Past and Present*. Lippincott, Philadelphia 1926; Batsford, London 1930.

Weale, J. (Ed.) *London Exhibited in 1851*. J. Weale, London 1851.

Shops Adburgham, A. *Shops and Shopping*. George Allen & Unwin, London 1964.

Benson, S. H. Ltd. *The Golden Jubilee of a Great Business*. Lipton Ltd., London 1948.

Boswell, J. (Ed.) *J. S. 100, The Story of Sainsbury's*. J. Sainsbury Ltd., London 1969.

Building News, The. London 1864.

Davis, D. *A History of Shopping*. Routledge & Kegan Paul, London 1966.

Delasseux, V., and Elliott, J. *Street Architecture*. John Weale, London 1855.

Greig, David Ltd. *The Story of a Family Firm, 1870–1970*. London 1970.

Huggett, R. *Shops*. Batsford, London 1969.

Mathias, P. *Retailing Revolution*, Longmans, London 1967.